ALASKAN JOB

The Disciplined Pursuit of Greatness

A. R. WEISSER

WESTBOW°
PRESS
A DIVISION OF THOMAS NELSON
& ZONDERVAN

Scripture quotations taken from the New American Standard Bible®,
Copyright © 1960, 1962, 1963, 1968, 1971, 1972, 1973, 1975, 1977, 1995
by The Lockman Foundation. Used by permission. (www.Lockman.org)

WestBow Press books may be ordered through booksellers or by contacting:

WestBow Press
A Division of Thomas Nelson & Zondervan
1663 Liberty Drive
Bloomington, IN 47403
www.westbowpress.com
1 (866) 928-1240

ISBN: 978-1-4908-7032-8 (sc)
ISBN: 978-1-4908-7034-2 (hc)
ISBN: 978-1-4908-7033-5 (e)

Library of Congress Control Number: 2015902649

Print information available on the last page.

WestBow Press rev. date: 02/24/2015

To my wife, Jenny,
who has graciously supported me in my efforts to
become greater than I once was, thank you.

And to my big brother, Jason,
who pestered me about writing this book;
here it is.

Contents

About the Author

I was born in Homer, Alaska, the third child of a Bible school teacher and part-time carpenter and the grandson of real-life homesteaders. When my family swelled to eight, my parents sensed God's calling to go to the Philippines as missionaries. Rejected by every agency because of their family size and delayed by a brother born with a major heart defect, my family finally moved to Manila as independent missionaries with a family of eleven. Once in the field, our family topped out at fifteen. Yes, I have eight brothers and four sisters. I am not sure why my parents stopped there, but no one seemed to hold it against them. After more than twenty-five years, my parents are still serving their Christ by helping blind Filipinos today.

When I was a junior at Faith Academy (a missionary kid school in Manila), a beautiful girl named Jenny asked me to a Sadie Hawkins banquet. Over time I learned to appreciate her other qualities. After graduation I went back to Alaska and attended a small Bible school for two years, and then that beautiful girl and I were married.

After two years of marriage, we moved to Chicago, where I enrolled at Moody Bible Institute for four years and worked summers as a commercial fishing vessel captain in Bristol Bay, Alaska. In 2005 I accepted a ministry opportunity as a youth pastor, and we moved back to Alaska with a one-year-old baby girl and number-two child on the way. In 2008 I was invited to colead a church plant endeavor in the town of my birth, and that has kept me busy since. As the ministry of Church on the Rock Homer has grown, so has my family; I have three sons and three daughters, each one amazing.

I have four ministry degrees from Alaska Bible Institute, Moody Bible Institute, and Columbia International University. And I am currently working on a fifth. School is a discipline for me. I study to avoid the mental lethargy that comes so naturally to me. Much of what you read in the following pages is the fruit of that learning.

Foreword

"Disciplined Productivity." I'll never forget how boring these words first seemed to me.

As new church planters in a small, seaside Alaskan community, Aaron and I had been discussing the core values we felt were essential to the health and vitality of the church we had launched. It became apparent to me that Aaron was quite determined that we should include "Disciplined Productivity" as one of those core values. To be honest, if it didn't hinder me from preaching, going to coffee with parishioners and building relationships with those far from Christ (while surfing of course), Aaron could be as "productively disciplined" as he wanted. I'll have fun, you be disciplined...I liked it!

Over the years I have come to the realization (albeit slowly and painfully) that my disinterest in discipline had very little to do with my "zest for life" and more to do with my inability to envision the kind of person I wished to become and to chart a course that would lead me there.

I've watched as my "church planting cohort" pursued, with a discipline rarely observed, the development of his own character as a husband, a father, a leader, a man. His desire to be a man of whom God could say, "Have you considered my servant...Aaron?" has been nothing short of compelling to our church, to our community, to me. (He can also leap over buildings in single bound!)

I say all of that to say this; it would be difficult for me to imagine someone whom I know so well and yet respect more than the author of the book you hold in your hands. I assume the character of the author matters to you as it does to me. I personally don't need another "sucker punch book" on "how to live my life" from a sucker who isn't even in the fight. I can say with certainty, that not only is Aaron in the fight, but he has seen some astounding victories along the way.

Aaron and I have weathered some storms together (both literally and figuratively), and I know with great confidence that the principles laid out in the pages ahead are far more than mere hypothetical and hollow rhetoric. Rather, what is set forth in the narrative before you has been the observable, disciplined, and fruitful pursuit of my dear friend.

I want you to know that the rich insight and thoughtful approach Aaron brings to Job 29 is something I have personally benefitted from and routinely borrowed in my disciple-making efforts. I have every confidence that as you examine the character of Job in the pages ahead, you will find yourself compelled to live the "examined life" just as I have.

My hope and prayer is that you will discover that a disciplined pursuit of Christ-like character yields both a present and eternal harvest beyond your grandest expectations and may you also come to truly know that our "light momentary affliction is preparing for us an eternal weight of glory beyond all comparison". II Corinthians 4:16 ESV

Enjoy,
Jonathan Walker
Lead Pastor, Church on the Rock – Wasilla, AK

Introduction

In each of the places I have lived, God has been present with me and has led me toward Himself and His plan. My personal stories take place in Alaska, Chicago, and Manila. But the contents of this devotional stem from my first real encounter with the presence of God in one particular place. I was a seventeen-year-old Bible school student, and I was doing what any good Bible school student would do; I was arguing with God about something I felt He was asking me to do.

Across the hall from my dorm room was Steve Landau. Steve had recently shared a devotional study about gossip. After he shared, I felt urged by the Holy Spirit to go and ask Steve to pray for me and my gossip problem. But I didn't want to. I didn't have a gossip problem. It was more of an occasional misstep. Besides, asking someone to pray for your problems is embarrassing. Surely God did not need Steve's help in dealing with my weakness. I would keep this issue to myself.

After a few days of putting it off, the conviction of the Holy Spirit was becoming unbearable. I was sitting at my desk in my room late one night, attempting to get my Bible school homework done, but the Holy Spirit was making that impossible. Bible school assignments are so much easier than obeying God's voice. As I argued, a Scripture reference came to mind. It was Job 23:4. I did not know what this verse said and thought it was odd that such a specific thought was in my brain. So I turned to Job 23:4 and read, "I would present my case before Him and fill my mouth with arguments." I was dumbfounded. So I got up from my desk, walked across the hall, and asked Steve Landau to pray for me and my gossip problem.

When I returned to my room that night, I had a powerful sense of God's presence there with me. As I prayed a prayer of repentance, God led me to another passage of Scripture—this time an entire chapter. I sensed that God was showing me the kind of man He was inviting me to become. But my unwillingness to listen to Him would disqualify me from this future. After all, insubordination is akin to witchcraft and idolatry (1 Samuel 15:23).

This devotional is a study on the chapter I read that night. At the time I thought maybe I was something special. Since then I have realized that this is God's desire for every man. In my own aspirations to become the man God wants me to be, I have gone back to this chapter for nearly twenty years now. Its guidance has been rich. I hope this study will be rich for you. And I trust that twenty years from now, you will still be working out its application in your own time and place.

Disciplined Pursuit

This is a book about being awesome. My quest to accomplish something truly awesome began early in life. I went after it pretty hard. One occasion in particular was so promising I *knew* it was going to be awesome well in advance. I could feel it in my bones. I was on the verge of a truly epic moment.

I was thirteen at the time and was undergoing changes that had stirred within me a growing fascination. All boys go through it. It had begun as a quiet but powerful urge a few years previous and now was in full expression, invading my otherwise-innocent daydreams. Yes. All men know what I am talking about. I was now unabashedly and passionately attracted to explosives. From the core of who I was as a young man, I wanted to blow stuff up. And I did.

Growing up for part of my life on the mission field in the mega-city of Manila, I had access to cheap explosives in the form of fireworks. These were the kind of fireworks that you can't buy over the counter in this country. Okay, so they weren't exactly sold over the counter in Manila either. You had to ask for them by name, and then they appeared—brown triangles about the size of a grilled cheese sandwich cut diagonally in two with a long red fuse. They were called Super Lolos, which essentially means Super Grand Daddies. They were awesome. And loud.

My plan had been fomenting since I had come to possess a piece of bamboo that was about four inches in diameter and roughly three and a half feet long. Bamboo is an intensely sturdy material, and it seemed automatic that this piece of material would make a fantastic cannon. Our home in Manila was surrounded by concrete block wall, on the back side of which was a large, overgrown empty lot. My heart palpitated at the thought of being able to launch projectiles over that wall and into the foliage of the lot next door. If I could reach all the way across this lot onto the roof of the next house, even better.

The concept of a cannon is fairly simple: a large tube stuffed with explosive powder, followed by wadding, followed by a projectile. No problem. I had my Super Lolos, some old rags, and a large rock that fit down into the bamboo stick perfectly.

Of course this kind of epic adventure should never be embarked upon alone, so I talked Levi and David, two of my younger brothers, into giving me a hand. The cannon had been loaded, and the fuse was ready to light. After failing to find a good location to affix our big gun, it seemed reasonable that the three of us would hold the barrel firmly while firing it off. Surely the recoil would not exceed the strength of three enthusiastic preteen boys.

I remember it so well: the cool concrete pebbled patio on my feet, the dark sky of endless opportunity, the excitement of joining with the ranks of castle-demolishing armies of centuries past mixed with the sheer terror of being discovered by my parents before our test firing was complete. On the count of three, I would light the red string and we would behold the majesty. Three … two … one. And boom.

The unfortunate thing about explosive experiments is that the culminating moment is rather brief. The gap of time between *prior to* the explosion and the state of emergency immediately following is imperceptibly small. Really there is less than a hair's width between serene calm and panicked hysteria. A skydiver with a failed parachute at least has a few moments to prepare emotionally for the pending disaster. Not so with cannons.

The cannon exploded. Literally. As in the whole cannon was blown into bits in our hands, like so many bamboo toothpicks.

Because the blast was simultaneously blinding and deafening, my senses were particularly tuned into the strange and prickly sensation I was experiencing everywhere my skin had been exposed, like a thousand bee stings all at once.

What brought me back to my awareness of the world around me was the sound of my screeching brother. *"My face, my face, my face, it's gone! My face is gone!"* I couldn't tell if his face was actually gone, because he was covering it with his clenched hands. I think he was clasping it in an attempt to save what was left. I had never seen someone lose his face before, but I felt this was bad. I tried shouting over his screams, *"Move your hands!"* but he continued to clench his faceless skull and holler about his face that was gone. *I hope my parents aren't hearing this*, I thought to myself. *"Move your hands!"* More screeching. *"Hold still."*

I pried his hands from his face for a close-up inspection and was relieved to see that it was all still there. David still had his face, and we still had ours. And our hands. Mostly our hearing was gone. And our skin felt tingly. The rock lay on the ground at our feet, looking only disappointed at the flight cancelation. The search for awesomeness was thwarted once again.

As I have aged, my quest to accomplish something truly great has grown more sophisticated, more mature, and more focused on eternal priorities. Thank goodness. The whole explosive trip would have proved costly over time, I imagine. (Think *The Hurt Locker* minus any meaningful motivation.) In this quest, I have learned to draw on the example of others. But let's be honest—those examples can be hard to come by. I'm looking for someone who is truly awesome but awesome in a way that I can both relate to and aspire to—someone inspiring but not alienating.

A Compelling Example

The purpose of this devotional is to share with you the best and most helpful example I have ever come across—a nearly perfect example. According to God Himself, "There is no one like him on the earth, a blameless and upright man, fearing God and turning away from evil" (Job 1:8). This nearly perfect example is the man Job. I believe there is no account of any man in all of Scripture that gives us a more descriptive look into the life of a righteous man than that of Job. When you consider God's description, it seems safe to say that Job was pretty much the man. Furthermore, Job is someone we can look to as an example of what it means to live life as a man of God right now. From what you remember about the story of Job, that may be confusing. Let me explain.

The book of Job only accounts for a very brief period of time in the life of Job. We see him just as he receives the terrible news of loss and destruction, and then we watch him briefly as he processes this traumatic experience with a few friends who were of no help at all. But what was Job's life like *before* Job 1:1 that led God to say to His heavenly friends, "There is no one like him on the earth"? That's the story I want to hear. Well, there is good news; in the twenty-ninth chapter of Job, we have that description.

Job 29 is a rather detailed and amazing description of the manliest man you will ever read about. I realize that guys like Abraham, Joseph, and David were all pretty awesome men we know about from Scripture. And yet these guys all had a rather specific calling that is quite a bit different than ours. Well, far different from mine for sure. Furthermore, none of them received the accolades from God that Job did. Job was an incredible man. But most importantly, he was a man just like us. Job wasn't a nomadic, wife-swapping patriarch like Abraham, a dream-weaving jailbird turned number two to pharaoh like Joseph, or a giant-slaying, harp-playing king like David. No. Job was a guy with a job, a ministry, a wife, some kids, and a hometown. Job was a lot like you and me … just way manlier. He was a regular guy but an incredible one.

Values & Discipline

This book is an examination of the simple and yet profound details of Job's life. Through this study you are going to discover that there is one primary thing that sets Job apart from the rest of the pack. I'll give you a hint: it was his disciplined habits. For the purpose of this study, I will define discipline as: *the ability to turn convictions into habits.*

Men who say they value their walk with God, their commitment to their wives, and their role in their children's lives are really not uncommon. Many of us know what we *should* value and what we *want* to value and yet never turn these convictions into habits in our lives. If you say you value the Word of God but have never developed the discipline to make reading the Word a habit in your life, bad news: you are self-deceived. Yeah, it's a cold truth, but it's true. If you say watching football is not the highest priority in your life and yet watching football is the only thing you never fail to do, you're fooling yourself. If watching the game is habitual and reading the Word is not, guess what is more valuable to you? I'm not talking about quantity of time. *I'm talking about priorities expressed through practical commitments.* The truth is this:

> *The habits of your life*
> *reflect what you value.*

In fact, habits are infallible in their testimony. If you work all the time and neglect your family, it is because you value work more than you do your family. Are you getting the picture? We tend to comfort ourselves by saying noble things like, "If it ever came down to it and I had to choose between my family and my work, I would choose my family without hesitation." Fantastic. And although it sounds inspiring, by the time you are actually faced with such a drastic decision, it's probably too late.

You see, we almost never have to choose to abandon one or the other. Yet daily we choose to prioritize one or the other. Daily we invest in what we love. Daily we broadcast to everyone around us what is important to us. Daily we choose. This is the *much* harder decision. This is what separates the men from the boys. This is the difference between men who are great and men who want to be great.

In this study we are going to examine ten habits of Job's life that made him who he was. In each of these habits you are going to be challenged to "discipline yourself for the purpose of godliness" (1 Timothy 4:7b). "Godliness is profitable for all things, since it holds promise for the *present life* and also for the *life to come*" (1 Timothy 4:8b emphasis added). You are going to be inspired by the life of Job as you study, and yet if that inspiration doesn't lead you to discipline, there will be no profit either in this life or in the life to come. The question you must ask as you examine these ten habits is this:

> *How will I develop this as an observable*
> *and consistent habit of my life?*

In other words, if my life were to undergo an activity audit, would there be any evidence that I spend my time investing in the things I claim to be most important? Would the findings of that independent auditor match the answers I give to the question, "What do you value?" If I never said a word, would that auditor come up with an answer I was comfortable with?

Rare Tenacity

If you were to sign up for army ranger boot camp today, you would discover very quickly that they have one goal in mind: to make you quit. They would stretch you to the limit of what you can physically, mentally, and emotionally handle for weeks on end and then dare you to quit. Why? Because they want you to quit. They want you to quit *before* you become an army ranger because they can't afford for you to quit after.

Army rangers have nothing on Job. If you want to become a great man of God, it will push you to your limit. For a period of time, especially at the beginning, it will feel like a soul-crushing grind. At times it will drain you of everything and then a little more. And many quit along the way. In fact, *most* quit. "The way is narrow that leads to life, and there are few who find it" (Matthew 7:14). *But*! It is also the pathway to a life that matters. Although it feels you are losing your life, you are really finding it (Matthew 16:25). Great men of God all realize that the price only seemed steep at the time, but the reward has been more than worth it. Great men never feel bad for themselves. They only feel bad for those who didn't make the cut.

Most army ranger recruits don't finish boot camp. Reading through this study will not make you into a man of God. Turning these ideas into disciplines will. If you read this devotional for inspiration, you've wasted your time. As you read each chapter, you will have an assignment to go and do. The doing is the part that matters. Honestly, it's going to take a while to adopt these disciplines. If you add one of the ten after the first read, I'm proud of you. Don't worry—this book will be here when you are ready to add another.

As we begin, take a moment and read through Job 29. Don't worry, we will come back and pick it apart later, but for now just get a feel for it:

JOB 29

And Job again took up his discourse and said,

Oh that I were as in months gone by, as in the days when God watched over me; when His lamp shone over my head, *and* by His light I walked through darkness; as I was in the prime of my days, when the friendship of God *was* over my tent; when the Almighty was yet with me, *and* my children were around me; when my steps were bathed in butter, and the rock poured out for me streams of oil! When I went out to the gate of the city, when I took my seat in the square, the young men saw me and hid themselves, and the old men arose *and* stood. The princes stopped talking and put *their* hands on their mouths; the voice of the nobles was hushed, and their tongue stuck to their palate. For when the ear heard, it called me blessed, and when the eye saw, it gave witness of me, because I delivered the poor who cried for help, and the orphan who had no helper. The blessing of the one ready to perish came upon me, and I made the widow's heart sing for joy. I put on righteousness, and it clothed me; my justice was like a robe and a turban. I was eyes to the blind and feet to the lame. I was a father to the needy, and I investigated the case which I did not know. I broke the jaws of the wicked and snatched the prey from his teeth. Then I thought, "I shall die in my nest, and I shall multiply *my* days as the sand. My root is spread out to the waters, and dew lies all night on my branch. My glory is *ever* new with me, and my bow is renewed in my hand." To me they listened and waited, and kept silent for my counsel. After my words they did not speak again, and my speech dropped on them. They waited for me as for the rain, and opened their mouth as for the spring rain. I smiled on them when they did not believe, and the light of my face they did not cast down. "I chose a way for them and sat as chief, and dwelt as a king among the troops, as one who comforted the mourners."

There is a lot in there. And we are going to unpack
it all in explicit detail.

So buckle up.
Let's get to work.

Walk with God's Light

The First Discipline

> When His lamp shone over my head, and by His light I walked through darkness. (Job 29:3)

This discipline is pretty simple, yet many men never bother. Notice the description of Job. Job did not look *at* a light; he looked *with* a light. The light was positioned above him, and it illuminated the area around him so he could confidently take steps forward. This is consistent with the psalmist, who said, "Your word is a lamp to my feet and a light to my path" (Psalm 119:105).

Living life without the Word of God is like driving in the dark without headlights. I have driven the Alaskan-Canadian highway numerous times from Washington state to Alaska (the place of my birth and my current residence). It is an incredible drive, but one area in particular is pretty treacherous. Stone Mountain Provincial

Park is known both for its stunning, harsh beauty and for its danger to drivers. There are sections of very narrow, winding road with no shoulder and sheer vertical faces on either side—one side going straight up higher than I can see from my vehicle and the other side dropping off into nothingness below. The man who is too busy to read the Word is like the man who is too busy to replace his faulty headlights while driving through Stone Mountain Provincial Park at night. It's just a bad idea.

Driving in the dark through Stone Mountain is going to be hard on your vehicle. If you make it out alive, your vehicle is going to be in rough shape. Ignore God's Word, and you might make it out alive, but you are going to get good and banged up along the way. Lights are important.

If you are going to walk by the light of God, it will require three commitments.

Commitment 1
Hear the Word of God

If you are going to walk *with* the light of God's Word, you will need to know His Word. There is no discipline more foundational and nonnegotiable to your spiritual development than this one. Living your life based upon what you remember from Sunday school and last Sunday's sermon is not sufficient—not even close. You must read the Word of God.

Right now, as you read this, you might already be checking out because you have tried and failed before. It may be an area where you already feel a high degree of guilt. Isn't it weird that I can sit down to read the living Word of God in order to hear from the Creator of the universe, and after a couple of paragraphs, I can't even remember what I just read? Sometimes I don't even remember reading it! My eyeballs saw the words on the page, but my brain was blank.

If you, like many men, find it difficult to read the Word—or for that matter, to read anything—you have two options: you can determine to do whatever it takes to get better at it, or you can quit. A lot of men quit. Becoming an effective reader takes hard work.

"How can a young man keep his way pure? By keeping it according to Your word. With all my heart I have sought You; do not let me wander from Your commandments. Your word I have treasured in my heart, that I may not sin against You" (Psalm 119:9–11). This writer had determined to not only be in the Word but also to *fill* himself with the Word. He didn't just hope for it; he *sought* after it. If you need some additional help developing the discipline of regularly reading God's Word, check out the study tool at the back of this devotional. It is a simple tool that will help you get started no matter where you are.

Commitment 2
Understand Its Relevance

"By His light I walked." While I was working aboard a commercial fishing boat in Alaska's Prince William Sound at the age of seventeen, the captain asked me to navigate the boat back to Whittier boat harbor so that he could get some rest during the three-hour trip. This was the first time I had navigated a vessel on my own at night, so he reminded me on the chart where we were headed and to watch the radar. Just as he headed down to his bunk, he said, "You can probably just follow the lights of the other boats out in front of us. They will be headed back into town as well."

There was only one slight problem; none of those boats were headed to harbor. I kept us following those lights perfectly but failed to read the radar and get a very careful read on our location. (This was prior to GPS days.) While believing we were headed in the right direction, I ignored the radar, only to discover I was headed the wrong way. By the time I realized my mistake, we were miles off course and my captain was not amused. Lights in the distance are no substitute for good radar.

If we are going to be led by God's Word, we must not regard it as a light in the distance but rather as a light shining around us. We must work to understand the relevance of God's Word to our daily lives, not just our future lives. The Word of God is not a book about things far off or lights glimmering on the horizon. The Bible, like radar, speaks to my current realities and accurately describes my location so I can successfully navigate through anything.

Commitment 3
Make Necessary Changes

"I walked through darkness." Once we hear God's Word and understand its relevance to our lives, we must then commit to stepping in whichever direction God leads us. Job realized that without God's Word, he would be in the dark. Because of God's Word, he not only could see in the dark, but he also knew where he should walk. The reality is this: the landscape of your life is scattered with open pits, thorn bushes, and even wild beasts. You encounter these in your marriage, finances, family, and work. The messages of the culture will send you flying headlong into these threats. Yet these things should not surprise you or sneak up on you. After all, you have the light of God shining over your head so you know where to step even in the darkness.

Recently, I walked from my bedroom into the crawl space closet. It is called the crawl space closet because there is a large floor hatch that, when opened, leads down into our four-foot crawl space under the house. Beyond this hatch cover, in the back of my closet, is my tool box. This particular time, I strolled into the closet without first flipping the light on. Much to my dismay, the hatch had been left open. I don't know if you have ever fallen into a crawl space hatch before, but I discovered that it involves a lot of pain and some flesh wounds. The pain is preceded by a split second of terror. "Either the hatch is open or a black hole has opened in my closet!" I think a black hole would have been less bruising.

Remember, God's Word is a light. When, through God's Word, you realize that a certain decision will lead you into a pit, you adjust. You don't take that step. You change your plan. You change your mind. You make the necessary changes because you trust that if God says no or go, it's always in your best interest to obey.

If you have not mastered the discipline of being led by God's Word, you have two options: you can quit or you can double down. Don't quit. Make a plan. Put the plan on your schedule. If you need help, get help. Remember, boot camp has just begun. Don't drop out in the first round. Your plan to develop the habit of being led by God's Word must be specific, concrete, and actionable. Answer the questions on the following page and share your answers with someone else who will encourage you towards your goal. If you have been neglecting this habit for years, now is the time to make a change. If you are willing to do the hard work necessary, the habit of being in the Word of God can and will become central to your life.

Making It Happen

> When His lamp shone over my head, and by His
> light I walked through darkness. (v. 3)

**(Write down your answers, and discuss them with a
likeminded guy.)**

What obstacles have prevented me from mastering the discipline of
being led by God's Word in my own life?

What do I need to do to overcome these obstacles?

What practical steps am I going to take to implement this discipline
in my own life?

Prayer: God, help me to turn my passion for Your Word into a habit
of being led by Your Word. Give me the courage to overcome any
obstacle that stands in my way and the determination to make it
happen.

Enjoy Friendship with God

The Second Discipline

> As I was in the prime of my days, when the friendship
> of God was over my tent; when the Almighty was
> yet with me. (Job 29:4–5a)

If the first discipline is simple (keep in mind, I didn't say easy, just simple), this second discipline can be rather complicated. If you ask a man to write down five titles that describe his view of God, more than likely the title *friend* will not be on the list. If you were a fifteen-year-old girl, you may describe God as your best friend, but if you are a grown man, it is not as likely. More common terms would be *Savior*, *Lord*, *Master*, and maybe for the less reverent, *the big guy upstairs*. Men seem to connect more with the idea of God's power and authority than they do with the idea of His nearness and companionship. For some, singing songs about God's intimate affection is enough to give us cold sweats.

Much of our concept of God and the way in which we relate to Him stems from our relationships with our dads. There is, of course, one slight problem with this natural way of things; our dads are all sinners, and God is not. I work very hard to model God's character to my own kids, yet I realize that even in my best moments, I am a poor representation of Him.

If you find it difficult to enjoy God as a constant companion, I would suggest taking some time to evaluate your relationship with your own dad. Ask yourself which characteristics of your dad you have inappropriately projected on God. This is an important step in seeing God for who He really is. If you have struggled with disappointment or hurt in your relationship with your dad, I encourage you to utilize the dad worksheet at the back of this devotional.

The word *friendship* is defined as "attached to another by affection."[1] Not affection like, "I want to cuddle with that person," but affection like, "I really enjoying being around and doing stuff with that person." Let's break this down into three commitments that promote the discipline necessary for healthy friendship.

Commitment 1
Mutual Respect

I had a friend during my college years who was the worst kind of friend a guy can have. He was the kind of friend who was closer than a brother when it was beneficial for him and more distant than a stranger when it was not. He was the ultimate fair-weather friend but always talked as if we were best buds. I knew we weren't best buds and couldn't figure out why he continued to make that

---

[1]   "Friend." *Merriam-Webster.com*. Merriam-Webster, n.d. Web. 15 Jan. 2015. <http://www.merriam-webster.com/dictionary/friend>.

claim. It drove me nuts. I remember the feeling of disrespect when he would blow me off.

In other news, pretty much every guy I know has had at least one bad boss. I have. It doesn't matter how hard you work, they refuse to give you any respect for what you accomplish. They ignore your strengths and obsess over your weaknesses. It's demoralizing. When you finally decide to quit, they disrespect you even more.

There really is nothing that causes a man to lose interest in a relationship faster than disrespect. And for me, this was the crux of my dysfunctional friendship with God. Somewhere deep inside of me, I believed God didn't respect me because of my shortcomings. I knew He had no reason to respect me. I was a sinner. I believed that He was my disappointed boss, always focused on my inability to measure up. I believed this because I was always focused on my inability to measure up. And as a result I was the ultimate fair-weather friend, calling on God only when I felt I really needed Him and largely ignoring Him when I didn't.

The truth is God does respect us. Our friendship with Him is built on it. The gospel has made real friendship with Him possible by separating us from His judgment and bringing us into His love. I have the righteousness of Jesus, and God has no disrespect for Jesus. "No longer do I call you slaves, for the slave does not know what his master is doing; but I have called you friends, for all things that I have heard from My Father I have made known to you" (John 15:15). We have been invited into a friendship built on mutual respect. You need to hear this: God has no disrespect for His sons.

Commitment 2
Mutual Enjoyment

Once respect is established, we move on to enjoyment. If you are going to enjoy friendship with God, you must find it enjoyable to be with Him. It's a really simple and yet difficult question to ask ourselves: "Do I like being with God?" If you are rarely or never motivated to spend time with God, it's because you don't like Him as a friend.

Maybe, like me, you carry too much shame from your failures and you're embarrassed to be with Him. Maybe you are too self-righteous and think you don't need Him. Maybe you are consumed with your career and don't have time for Him. Maybe there are things in your life that you know aren't good and so you avoid Him. These are the four major barriers that kill enjoyment. There are others.

Whatever it is, you just don't enjoy Him. And unless you are *determined* to find enjoyment in that relationship, you probably never will. As David says, "Let all who seek you rejoice and be glad in You" (Psalm 40:16). Those who seek after God are the ones who find enjoyment in that relationship. If you really believe that you are just too far gone for Jesus to want a friendship with you consider the fact that He had a reputation for being a "friend of tax collectors and sinners" (Luke 7:34)! You might be just the kind of guy that He would want to hang out with!

If you have struggled to develop or maintain a prayer life, it is likely connected to enjoyment. It's hard to keep a conversation going with someone you don't like being around. Job was lamenting what seemed like a loss of friendship with his God. You don't miss someone you don't enjoy. The challenge is to seek God even before I find the relationship enjoyable. You can press through the hard work of getting to know God, believing that the relationship will grow more enjoyable, or you can quit because it's too hard. Saying that you love God more than anything while privately avoiding Him like the plague will not gain you points with anyone.

You should know that God enjoys you. "The Lord Your God is with You … He will take great delight in You … and will rejoice over you" (Zephaniah 3:17). Press on in your walk, committed to finding that same enjoyment in God that He finds in you. The next commitment will give you a pathway to press ahead.

Commitment 3
Mutual Experience

I remember the first time my dad gave me (what as a nine-year-old felt like) a legitimate job at his construction site. It was awesome. I was awesome. I was doing *real* work, and nothing could have been more exciting.

According to James 2:23, Abraham "believed God, and it was reckoned to him as righteousness and he was called the friend of God." He was not saying that Abraham mentally agreed with the claims of God. When he said that Abraham believed God, he was referring to Abraham's decision to go along with God's plan based upon God's promise. God showed up and said to Abraham, "I've got big plans for you, and you need to uproot and move to a land far away in order to be a part of the plan." And so Abraham did. Abraham and God embarked on a journey together. Men were made to work side by side, and God invites us to work alongside of Him.

It's unfortunate that relationship with God has been reduced to the occasional chitchat for many. It is meant to be much more. Job was not only lamenting the feeling of lost friendship, he was wrestling with a sense of isolation. Job was missing that sense of partnership he had enjoyed with God. We are called to a partnership with God. God has given us real tasks, some of which we will be looking at through this study. But these tasks are not meant to be done *for* Him. God doesn't actually need your help with anything (Acts 17:25). They are meant to be done *with* Him. Henry Blackaby made this point when he urged us to look around and find out what God is doing and then join Him.[2] If you want to really develop friendship with God, commit to pursuing mutual experiences with Him where the two of you are working side by side. Examine your life; is there any area of endeavor where you have a clear sense of

---

[2]   Henry Blackaby, Richard Blackaby & Claude King, *Experiencing God: Knowing and Doing the Will of God* (Nashville, TN: B&H Publishing, 2008).

needing God's help? If not, add such an endeavor. Go tackle a challenge that you know God wants but will fail miserably without His help. Go and partner with Him. If you haven't tried it, I can tell you from experience, it's awesome.

If you have not mastered the disciplined pursuit of friendship with God to the point that it has become truly enjoyable, you can quit or you can double down. Don't quit. Press through the hard work of friendship until you arrive at the enjoyable part of friendship. Implement a plan to build your friendship with God by investing consistent time in your relationship with Him. It is the most important investment you can make.

Making It Happen

> As I was in the prime of my days, when the friendship
> of God was over my tent; when the Almighty was
> yet with me. (v. 4–5a)

(Write down your answers, and discuss them with a likeminded guy.)

What obstacles have kept me from the enjoyment of friendship with God?

What do I need to do to overcome these obstacles?

What practical steps am I going to take to implement this discipline into my own life? *(Remember, friendship is developed over time.)*

Prayer: God, help me to learn the enjoyment of walking in friendship with You. Give me the courage to overcome any obstacle that stands in my way and the determination to make it happen.

Gather Your Family

The Third Discipline

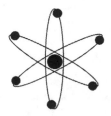

And my children were around me. (Job 29:5b)

In the remaining disciplines, Job is going to describe his outward life. If you pursue the next eight disciplines while neglecting the first two, there are two possible outcomes. Either you will become disillusioned and depressed because of the hard work required or you will become self-righteous and ultimately obnoxious as you impress yourself with yourself. Godly discipline is energized by the goodness of God and directed towards the glory of God. If you fight hardest for the first two, the other disciplines will require less effort. Now, it's time to move forward.

The language of this passage is essential. Observe the arrangement:

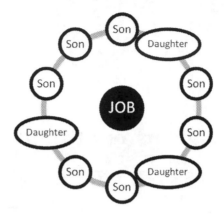

If you observed that the daughters are oval, nice work, but not relevant. In Job's description, he is the gravitational center of his family; he is the nucleus. Job is the gathering force around which the family comes together. *(And yes, he had ten kids.)* Fathers are meant to be leaders. Yet in our modern conception of family, dads are an afterthought. Dads are the unnecessary buffoons who are easily outsmarted and quickly discarded by their smart-mouthed twelve-year-olds because they aren't cool enough and just don't get it.

In remembering his deceased children, Job longs for the time when his kids were gathered around him. In order to lead our kids, we must move beyond incidental parenting and embrace intentional leadership. Incidental parenting describes my natural tendency to lead my kids only when there is an issue. "Don't do that." "Don't talk back." "Do what I asked." "You know better." Intentional leadership happens when I bring my kids around me for the purpose of guiding and modeling godly living. "Let me explain why we do this." "I would like it if you would join me while I do this."

This kind of leadership isn't natural to me. I am usually content to let my wife gather the family and then show up if it seems like something fun or to avoid feeling guilty for not showing up. This won't cut it. And in the long run it will produce very frustrating results. As a man and a father, I must lead. I must gather my family. This will require the following three commitments.

Commitment 1
Don't Be a Jerk

I believe there are two primary reasons kids avoid spending time with their dads. The first reason is because dads are overly critical and mean. If in your heart you find the immaturity of your kids to be annoying, your kids know it. They will by nature begin to either avoid you or work overly hard to impress you—both unhealthy options. This is why Paul warns dads, "Fathers, do not provoke your children to anger, but bring them up in the discipline and instruction of the Lord" (Ephesians 6:4). Sometimes I wonder if Paul meant to say, "Children, do not provoke your fathers to anger!"

Last year I was under my house fixing a plumbing problem that my kids had created. After spending hours trying to solve the issue, as a last-ditch effort, I cut the main sewer line in order to retrieve the offending object. I instructed my children in dogmatic terms: *"Do not use the plumbing."* With severed sewer pipe in my arms and realizing I didn't have the right tool to finish the job, I called a neighbor of mine who I thought might have the correct device. And then through the pipe I heard the echo of a distant flush. Sheer panic. In my spastic effort to realign the pipes before the deluge, I dropped my iPhone into the open sewer line right as the sewage came splashing down. Paul tells dads not to provoke their kids to anger because Paul knows kids will provoke their dads to anger.

Kids are irresponsible, immature, and self-centered by nature, not by choice. It's part of being a kid. As a father it can seem exhausting and irritating to explain the same simple concept to my child five thousand times. I can even get offended by their self-centered lack of respect. "If you roll your eyes at me one more time I'm gonna …" (Then I try and think of some consequence that will frighten them into submission.) But if I find myself intolerant of their "kidness" then I am in danger of driving them away and losing my opportunity to influence them. If I am controlled by kindness and gentleness, my family will want to be with me. If you are going to gather your family, you cannot act like a jerk.

Commitment 2
Don't Be a Wet Noodle

The second reason kids avoid their dads is because they have no respect for their leadership. This is the second part of Paul's statement: "But bring them up in discipline and instruction." There is a pervasive humanistic belief that kids intuitively know what's best for them. This is completely foolish, and it is not true. Kids can tell you a lot about *how* they learn but have little idea as to *what* they need to learn. If you ask my kids, they will tell you that lots of junk food, TV, and video games, along with no sleep and no school, is the best plan possible. You don't lead your kids by asking their permission or by catering to their childish whims. Believe it or not, always caving to what your kid wants actually makes them resent you.

Strong leadership requires the capacity to insist on what's best for your kids. I know it is not in my kids' best interest to let them punch someone in the ear when they don't get their way. If I allow this, they will find it very difficult to form friendships as adults. So I don't allow it. Every time it happens, there are consequences. My kids know I am unwavering in my commitment to help them overcome their selfish tendency to throw fits. As a result, they respect my leadership and gradually change.

Paul says that men who desire to be leaders in the church must be "good managers of their children and their own households" (1 Timothy 3:12). A good manager must be kind and must be confident to lead. As you gather your family, explain your biblical motives:

- We are going to eat together as a family (*gathering for relationship—love one another*).

- We are going to read God's Word together (*gathering to learn—God's Word is life*).
- We are going to pray together (*gathering to seek God—seek and you will find*).
- We are going to help our neighbor together (*gathering to serve—pure religion is to help those in need*).
- We are going to repair the fence together (*gathering to work—diligence has its reward*).

Then require happy participation.

Commitment 3
Meet Your Kids at Their Level

Once we have committed ourselves to lead our kids with kindness and with courage, we must then overcome our own boredom if we are ever going to connect with them. One of the things my kids love doing is playing games. It's a great way to gather the family for time together. Only one problem: the games they like are incredibly boring.

My oldest daughter's favorite game when she was younger was Sorry! I don't know if you have played Sorry! lately, so I'll refresh your memory. It's boring. And dumb. There is absolutely zero strategy involved. The players take turns rolling the dice for half an hour until someone wins. When my kids play, they insist on shaking the dice around in their hands for at least ten minutes before rolling. Apparently this improves their chances of getting a six. And to make it worse, about every other turn the dice careen off the table, across the floor, and into some impossible-to-reach cranny. I'm getting tired just writing about it.

Once again my natural tendencies get me in trouble here. My solution is to gather my kids to do the things I enjoy and then demand that they act like they are having fun. "Smile, everyone!"

There is a term for this. It's called selfishness. Or maybe I force them into activities that are really just unfulfilled dreams from my own childhood. Also selfish.

One of the basic truths of the gospel is that God came down to us and joined us at our level (Philippians 2). Christ lowered Himself. I assure you He made a greater sacrifice than you will as you meet your kids at their level. Part of effectively gathering your family is to tune into their needs and interests and to find enjoyment through facilitating their enjoyment.

In my house, one of the ways I gather my family is Thursday pizza night. I come home from work and make pizza for my family. I try to be creative in my work because surprisingly enough, pizza in a new shape is like pizza for the first time and is the coolest thing ever when you're a kid. After dinner we watch a movie together. It's a pretty simple plan—a weekly habit. And when it doesn't happen, my kids give me an earful. My kids expect me to gather my family. For some simple gathering ideas, check out the "Family Time" resource at the back of this devotional.

Developing the discipline of gathering your family will take some work over a period of time. But it must become a habit. If it is not something you have done, there may be some initial resistance. Your kids may tell you it's a dumb requirement. It will also require you to grow up as a leader and face your own shortcomings in this area. You have two choices. I think by this time you know what they are. You can do the hard work or you can quit. It's your choice. I would suggest that you don't quit. Just know this: God will help you as you seek His strength.

Making It Happen

And my children were around me. (v. 5b)

(Write down your answers and discuss them with a likeminded guy.)

What obstacles have kept me from taking the initiative to gather my family?

What do I need to do to overcome these obstacles?

What practical steps am I going to take to implement this discipline into my own life?

Prayer: God, give me the strength and wisdom to prioritize my family by gathering us together. Give me the courage to overcome any obstacle that stands in my way and the determination to make it happen.

Enjoy God's Abundance

The Fourth Discipline

When my steps were bathed in butter, and the rock
poured out for me streams of oil. (Job 29:6)

I remember as a ten-year-old boy standing on the beach in my
hometown in Alaska and picking up a ball of sticky crude oil that had
originated in the now-cracked hull of the Exxon Valdez oil tanker.
In an era where landowners in North Dakota are getting filthy rich
overnight by drilling for oil in their backyards and British Petroleum
can accidently pump hundreds of millions of gallons of oil into the
gulf of Mexico, this Scripture may need some context. Job was not
exactly drilling for crude. He was not Jed Clampett of the Beverly
Hillbillies. In his day and age, *edible* oil was a high commodity that
was likely made from olives. The last time I checked, edible oils are
made, not found. The process of making oil requires distilling the

oil from the olive fruit through a long cooking process. The same is true with butter. It is made, not found gushing from the ground as I mosey along. So why then does Job reminisce about oil pouring from rocks and butter gushing out of the ground?

Job is apparently using hyperbole to make a point. Oil was not only coming from rocks—it was coming from rocks in *streams*! Butter was not just in abundance on the table; it was literally flowing from the ground everywhere he walked. Job is making it clear to the listener that the abundance he experienced could not be explained naturally because oil and butter do not occur naturally. Yes, he was successful. Yes, he was business savvy. But he also understood that the abundance he experienced was abundance from God that defied logic. God was blessing Job beyond his abilities, and Job knew it. And Job was grateful for it. He did not pretend that God's abundant blessing was nothing to get excited about. *No!* Job said, "Man, those days were incredible!" In order to truly enjoy abundance, every man must learn the discipline of receiving everything good as *God's* abundance. The following commitments will help to shape your development of this discipline.

Commitment 1
All the Stuff Is from God

I find it amazing how selfish a kid can be. My four-year-old son discovered an old shirt belonging to his older brother at the bottom of one of his dresser drawers. My seven-year-old hadn't seen it or asked about it in months. And yet the moment he laid eyes on that shirt being worn proudly by his little brother, he was inconsolable. He had to have it. And so I intervened.

"Why are you making such a big deal over an old shirt?" I asked.

"Because I really want that shirt," he replied.

"But you haven't wanted that shirt for months. Why do you suddenly want it now?"

Without pausing, he dogmatically asserted, "Because it's mine!"

And like that, I had him cornered. "Where did you get that shirt?"

He paused and then shrugged.

"Did Mom buy it for you?"

He nodded.

"Whose money did she buy it with?"

At this point even his seven-year-old brain realized the trap I was laying for him.

He pointed at me silently, not wanting to verbally lend weight to my infallible point.

"If we bought you a shirt with our money and gave it to you, don't you think it would be okay to share your shirt with your brother?"

As silly as this whole interaction seems to me, I realize it is a parable of my own view of stuff. Rather than walking in the reality that everything I have comes from God, the moment I get stuff, I selfishly hold onto to it because I "need" it; because it's "mine"! Listen to what God says in Psalm 50:10–12: "For every beast of the forest is Mine, the cattle on a thousand hills. I know every bird of the mountains, and everything that moves in the field is Mine. If I were hungry I would not tell you, for the world is Mine, and all it contains." Job was not faking humility when he said, "The Lord gave and the Lord has taken away" in Job 1:21. He meant it. Everything he had, he received as coming from the Lord and ultimately belonging to the Lord. A righteous man must make the commitment to live as a steward of God's abundance, not as an owner. Everything I have is a gift from God.

Commitment 2
Do Not *Ever* Trust the Stuff

"Behold, the man who would not make God his refuge, but trusted in the abundance of his riches and was strong in his evil desire" (Psalm 52:7). Trusting in riches and strong in evil desire—as if the two go hand in hand. Yikes. Job made it very clear that this was not the case for him. "If I have put my confidence *in* gold, and called fine gold my trust … That too would have been an iniquity *calling for* judgment, for I would have denied God above" (Job 31:24, 28).

The challenge we face is that we naturally put our trust in the stuff. It happens without us even realizing it. But there is a surefire way to counteract this natural tendency. It really works; it's just really hard. The strategy is to regularly give the stuff away. That's right. Take your hard-earned cash and give it away. Give it to the needy. Give it to your church. Give it to missions. Just give it away somewhere. In doing so you will train your heart not to trust in the money in your wallet. And surprisingly, you will enjoy what you do have more because you are not holding onto it so tightly.

I recently spoke to a young fisherman who told me that he had decided before the fishing season to give 100 percent of his first day's income to the Lord. That is incredible. The first day of the season can be a huge catch. But this guy knew the danger of putting his trust in the stuff and preempted that potential. It's amazing how quickly the things you own begin to own you. This is not freedom; this is slavery. And many people today are willing slaves to their stuff. Developing the discipline of enjoying God's abundance requires the commitment to hold our things loosely. If you say you don't trust in all the stuff but you don't enjoy giving it away, guess what? You trust the stuff. For some of you, this is the first discipline that is really going to hurt. But don't worry, it won't be the last.

Commitment 3
Invest Now for later

If I were to ask you for a $100 loan with the signed agreement that tomorrow I would return that loan with 1,000,000 percent interest, to the degree that you believed I had the capacity to make good on my contract, you wouldn't hesitate. In fact, you would be freaking out. If you didn't have the $100 on you, I'm guessing you would get a hold of some cash and quickly. Hell's gates would not stop you from getting that $100 into my hands. Imagine going to sleep that night with the realization that tomorrow your hundred bucks was going to become a cool million. You wouldn't. You would lie awake until morning with your heart palpitating. If you had declined my offer and the word got out, you would be regarded as a madman. Your friends would look at you in disbelief. "What were you thinking!"

The Scriptures make it clear on more than a couple of occasions that we cannot possibly give away more than we will receive in return through Christ (Luke 18:29–30; Mark 10:29–30). We stand to receive a massive, exponential, eternal return on our investment when we are motivated by the sacrifice of Christ and live with the same sacrificial mind-set. Abundance is the end game for us who are in Christ (John 10:10). Imagine how perplexed the angels must be when they see us holding onto our dollar bills knowing that we are missing out on a ridiculous investing opportunity. It is exactly the security of the investment as guaranteed in the promises of God's Word that motivates us to invest while we still have time. The most enjoyable thing you can do with God's stuff is use it for God's purposes. This is what it means to enjoy God's abundance. It is the daily discipline of using your resources in the way God desires.

If you have not mastered the discipline of enjoying God's abundance, keep working at it. It is a difficult discipline for many to master and involves long-term planning, budgeting, and wise financial decision making. If you are stuck financially and want to get started with a better plan, use the "Money Managing" tool at the back of this devotional. The better you plan, the more you'll have, and the more you have, the more you can give. Now you have two choices. You can do the hard work or you can quit. Don't quit; the potential reward is far too great.

Making It Happen

> When my steps were bathed in butter, and the rock
> poured out for me streams of oil. (v. 6)

(Write down your answers, and discuss them with a likeminded guy.)

What obstacles have kept me from the learning to enjoy God's abundance according to God's plan?

What do I need to do to overcome these obstacles?

What practical steps am I going to take to implement this discipline into my own life?

Prayer: God, give me the capacity to receive from You and give back to You as a habit of my life. Give me the courage to overcome any obstacle that stands in my way and the determination to make it happen.

Pursue Honor

The Fifth Discipline

When I went out to the gate of the city, when I took
my seat in the square, the young men saw me and
hid themselves, And the old men arose and stood.
The princes stopped talking and put their hands on
their mouths; the voice of the nobles was hushed,
and their tongue stuck to their palate. (Job 29:7–10)

Honor is a funny thing. Every man alive possesses an innate
desire for it. Most men, if forced to choose, will choose honor over
companionship. The term *honor* means, "One whose worth brings
respect."[3] Put in other words, "You look up to me because I'm

---

3   "Honor." *Merriam-Webster.com*. Merriam-Webster, n.d. Web. 15 Jan.
     2015. <http://www.merriam-webster.com/dictionary/honor>.

awesome." Let's be honest—we all want someone else to look at something we've accomplished and say, "That's awesome." As a young teen I thought the pathway to becoming awesome would be to build my own cannon. The outcome was awesome but not in the way I had imagined. Your pathway has likely been different.

Here's a fun fact: the average age of the most frequent video game purchasers is thirty-five. And they are mostly male. The most common genre of these games? Epic conflict. (If you're not a gamer, just bear with me for a sec.) Truth be told, real life seems to offer little opportunity to conquer the world, and the pathway to honor and esteem seems at best hidden and at worst, completely gone. So we head off into the land of make believe, where we conquer to our hearts' content.

What we end up with is a cheap feeling of honor and esteem that is disconnected from any real-world accomplishment. The evil we defeat isn't real. The woman we rescue isn't real. The badges of merit are not real. The only thing real is the hours wasted and my growing disconnection from the life of honor God intended for me. Real honor requires a little more investment to obtain than do virtual merit badges.

There is a legitimate pathway to honor. And if you are interested in fully realizing God's purposes for you, you will need to walk this path. Truth is you were made for this path. God intends for you to pursue honor as a habit of your life. The following three commitments will help you get on track.

Commitment 1
Every Man Was Made for Honor

The first thing we must get straight in our minds is that the pursuit of honor is not an inherently ungodly one or a selfish one. Honor is God's intent for man, not just some demand that an out-of-control egomaniac decided he couldn't live without. The fact that many pursue honor through pretentious manipulation or outright power struggles doesn't make that pursuit wrong. The question is not *whether* we should pursue honor but *how*. This is God's description of man's position of honor as recorded in Psalm 8:5–6 "You made him a little lower than the heavenly beings and crowned him with glory and honor. You made him ruler over the works of your hands; you put everything under his feet." Amazing. God has granted us honor.

A couple thousand years ago, the disciples of Jesus tangled in an honor feud to determine which of them was the greatest of all. In a very unfortunate moment in one such chest-beating exchange, certainly to the embarrassment of James and John, their mother jumped into the fray on their behalf. In Matthew 20 she personally petitioned Jesus to show preference for her boys by placing them in a position of honor. The other ten disciples were not amused.

While we may be a little too polished to engage in such a dispute, we seek superiority in more subtle ways. But what I find fascinating about these exchanges, which are recorded in each of the gospels, is that Jesus did not repudiate their desire for honor. Jesus *directed* their pursuit of honor but did not attempt to discredit it. He gave the disciples a pathway to honor and also described an inappropriate pathway to honor. Let's take a look at both while keeping in mind this truth: God intended you for a position of honor. You shouldn't feel weird about going after it.

Commitment 2
Honor Must Not Be Grasped

First let's deal with the inappropriate path to honor. This path really works for some people, but it's the wrong kind of honor. Verse 25 says, "You know that the rulers of the Gentiles lord it over them, and *their* great men exercise authority over them." It's a fairly simple strategy: use whatever power you have to demand respect from those who have less power than you.

Want to be honored at work? No problem. Just treat everyone beneath you like minions and demand they treat you with respect. Want to be honored at home? No problem. Assert yourself as the king of your mansion and demand that your wife submit while demanding that your kids respect you. Anytime you are treated with disrespect, just fly off the handle and make everyone afraid to treat you that way again. The more unpredictable you are, the more those around you will *act* like they respect you. Of course, they are pretending because they really fear and resent you.

Notice Job's action in this passage: "I took my seat in the square." Wow. Job showed up in a public location and sat down. The setting is not one where Job had designated authority that we know of. This wasn't a corporate meeting where he was the CEO. He was not the mayor. There was no bailiff announcing his arrival to the bench: "All rise for the honorable Job." In any controlled setting, if you have authority, you can demand respect. You can "lord it over" those beneath you. In the city square, things are not the same. And yet the arrival of Job prompted the honorable response of the other men, both young and old, who were present. They honored him of their own accord because they felt him deserving. The honor Job received was an honor he pursued in the same manner of every righteous man who has lived. He pursued it according to God's pathway. This is the third commitment.

Commitment 3
Humility Is the Pathway to Honor

In simple terms, the pathway up is down. "Before destruction the heart of man is haughty, but humility *goes* before honor" (Proverbs 18:12). "A man's pride will bring him low, but a humble spirit will obtain honor" (Proverbs 29:23). This principle is reiterated constantly throughout Scripture, including in the previously mentioned discussion between Jesus and His disciples. "It is not this way among you, but whoever wishes to become great among you shall be your servant, and whoever wishes to be first among you shall be your slave; just as the Son of Man did not come to be served, but to serve, and to give His life a ransom for many" (Matthew 20:26–28). I would define this kind of humility in the following way: the disposition of caring more about meeting the needs of others than the needs of oneself.

The challenge for me is that I often use this legitimate pathway in an illegitimate way to grasp for honor—a violation of the second commitment. I will do something to meet the need of my wife and then quietly fume if she doesn't give me some kind of positive feedback. This is the opposite of humility. My motivation in serving her needs is quickly discovered as covert operation to meet my own need for honor. I only did it to get noticed, and when I don't get noticed, I realize that I am unmotivated to continue serving her in the same way. True humility is *more* motivated by the needs of another. This means that the enjoyment I find is directly derived from the act of serving, not exclusively in what I get in return. Is it nice to have a positive response? Yes. Do I have to have it? No, not if I have embraced humility.

Jesus was preaching what He would ultimately practice to an extent that we will never have to. According to Philippians 2, He set aside all of the honor and privilege due Him as the Son of God and humbled Himself by becoming a man *so* He could serve our need by dying in order to set us free. Because of His willingness to humble Himself, "God highly exalted Him" (Philippians 2:9). Jesus not only explained to us the pathway to honor, but He also showed us. And here is His promise to those who choose the same pathway: "God gives grace to the humble" (James 4:6). When you choose the pathway of humility, God becomes your ally in that choice and enables you to stay on course.

You may be wondering at this point what evidence there was in Job's life that he chose the path of humility in order to obtain honor. We are going to examine this evidence in the next couple of disciplines. As you work to develop the discipline of pursuing honor through a life of humility, it will *feel* very costly at times and it will *be* very costly all the time. This is a tough one for me because it is so counterintuitive. I am not a humble servant by nature. But trust Him. Don't give up. He will lift you up as you lay your life down.

Remember, we are not talking about feelings. It doesn't really matter if you *feel* humble. We are talking about disciplines. The discipline of pursuing honor through humbly laying my life down should be an observable habit of my life. Someone from the outside looking in should say, "Wow, look at him give his life away!" It begins this way. Start with one block of time—let's say Monday morning from the time you wake up until you leave your house for work. How could you turn that block of time into an opportunity to serve? Once you've got that down, move on to another block. You are going to be stretched if you commit to this, but don't quit. Press on in God's strength. What will your path to honor look like this week?

Making It Happen

> When I went out to the gate of the city, when I took my seat in the square, the young men saw me and hid themselves, And the old men arose and stood. The princes stopped talking and put their hands on their mouths; the voice of the nobles was hushed, and their tongue stuck to their palate. (v. 7–10)

(Write down your answers, and discuss them with a likeminded guy.)

What obstacles have kept me from pursuing honor according to God's pathway of humility?

What do I need to do to overcome these obstacles?

What practical steps am I going to take to implement this discipline into my own life?

Prayer: God, give me the courage to pursue humility as Your legitimate pathway to honor. Give me the courage to overcome any obstacle that stands in my way and the determination to make it happen.

Pursue Mercy

The Sixth Discipline

> For when the ear heard, it called me blessed, and
> when the eye saw, it gave witness of me, because
> I delivered the poor who cried for help, and the
> orphan who had no helper. The blessing of the one
> ready to perish came upon me, and I made the
> widow's heart sing for joy. I was eyes to the blind
> and feet to the lame. I was a father to the needy. (Job
> 29:11–13, 15–16a)

And now Job is going to really lay down the gauntlet for those who
are tempted to doubt his righteous stature. In the quest for the cup,
at this point it occurs to me that Job's car, which up until now I was
feeling confident I may be able to keep up with, has in fact already
lapped me. This guy is killing it. In the next five disciplines, Job

will go from great guy to superhero. If you doubted that Job pursued honor on the path of humility, he's about to prove his case. And here's the deal: you can do the same. Of course that will require hard work and not everyone is up to that.

With this next discipline things can start to get messy. Engaging the world with all of its problems is messy. It's exhausting and at times confusing. Shortly after moving overseas, my parents decided to proactively connect their kids with ministry opportunities. It was close to Christmastime, so they thought it would be a cool idea to have us hand out apples to the street kids living near our home. I too thought it sounded like fun. Who doesn't want to hand out free stuff! About two minutes into our ministry initiation, we were mobbed. And the mob began to physically crush us. My dad had to fight his way to us in order to rescue us from the riot. Apples were flying through the air. We all survived the few minutes of insanity but agreed for a different approach in the future. Like I said, this kind of ministry can be messy.

If you are going to embrace the "true religion" described in James 1:27 and show mercy to those with desperate needs, it will require three firm commitments on your part. It's time to go all in.

Commitment 1
Overcome the Awkwardness

Let's be honest, dealing with poverty, isolation, death, illness, and injury is not a fun assignment. These were the exact people Job was dealing with. When typhoon Ondoy hit my once hometown of Manila in 2009, dropping eighteen inches of rain in twenty-four hours, big sections of the city were devastated.

At the time I was living back in Alaska and decided to take a team a week after the storm to help rebuild. On the first day we were there, we stopped to visit a family whose home had been knocked flat. This family was already living in poverty before the storm, and when we found them, they were camping beneath the tiny roof of their collapsed home. To make matters more desperate, the father of this family was blind, the mother was slightly crippled, and their child was blind as well. As we stood there, mouths gaping, taking in the impossibility of their situation, I remember feeling like a loser. What could I do for them? What could I say? It was awkward just being there. It's always the same for me in any similar situation.

Whether it be meeting someone who has just lost a loved one, someone who has found himself in a crippling financial situation, someone about to have a limb amputated, or someone living in complete isolation in a home that reeks of loneliness, the feeling is always the same. I don't know why I feel stupid in those situations because: 1. I'm a pastor and 2. I'm not prone to feeling stupid. But I do. And my flesh would send me away from these situations to avoid that awkward, helpless feeling.

But I can't stay away. The gospel doesn't give us the choice of staying away. I must confront my fear of my own weakness and the awkwardness of not knowing how to help and just dive in head first anyway. It would be nice to just pray for them from a distance or maybe even send a card and say, "Praying for you." Praying allows me to feel like I've involved myself without physically involving myself. But according to James 2:15–16, "If a brother or sister is without clothing and in need of daily food, and one of you says to them, 'Go in peace, be warmed and be filled,' and yet you do not give them what is necessary for their body, what use is that?" If I *can* get involved then I *should* get involved. Job was a man who showed up when people were hurting the most and got involved. Yes, it can be awkward, and yes, you will survive the awkwardness. But let's take it a step further.

Commitment 2
Go and Find the Needs

One of the most important aspects of the gospel that must sink in to our psyche is the concept of initiative. This is spelled out in

Romans 5:8 "For Christ demonstrates His love for us in that while we were still sinners Christ died for us." If God had waited for us to beg and plead for a Savior, we would have no Savior. But He didn't. God initiated meeting our needs before we ever asked. He came and found us in the darkness that was the deception of our own sin. Have you ever been in a completely helpless situation? Or worse, have you ever been completely helpless and realized no one was coming to help?

As an eight-year-old I took a trip halibut fishing with my dad, my brother and sister, my uncle, and my cousin. It was a little boat and halibut fishing happens in deep water, so we were a few miles from shore. As the day rolled, on a thick fog bank rolled in and enveloped our small craft. This was in the days before GPS and this boat had no radar, so my dad decided that we would fish as long as the nearest boat fished and then we would follow them home.

As evening approached, the other boat pulled anchor, and we followed suit and began following its wake. As it turned out, we were following a boat that also had no radar. Within minutes we realized this boat was leading us in loop-de-loops. For the adults this meant the inconvenience of a lousy night's sleep on a dank little boat. For an eight-year-old boy, this was the first experience of a profound hopelessness. We did not know where we were, and no one else knew where we were either. We were totally lost in a gradually darkening sea of gray. What if no one ever found us! What if the fog never lifted? What about dinner? How would I sleep without my pillow? I could not fight the clammy grip of despair. I peered into the dark, foggy nothingness trying to will a search vessel into existence. It didn't come.

For many people this is their daily experience in regard to their basic needs. Lost in a sea of fog that is their helpless state, they peer into the dark night, attempting to will a solution into existence. In our case, the foggy night eventually turned into a beautiful morning, and twenty minutes later, we were back to harbor. For some, the morning never comes and the fog persists. What if they were to peer into the fog and see your face appear? Would this not be a miracle? Would you not be, in that moment, the answer to all of their prayers? Job was. "Have I eaten my morsel alone, and the orphan has not shared it? But from my youth he grew up with me as with a father, and from infancy I guided her" (Job 31:17–18).

So how did Job find these people? It doesn't say. But he did. If you are going to be the righteous man God has called you to be, you will have to find them as well. Don't say, "Can I find them?"; say, "How will I find them?" And then find them.

Commitment 3
Develop a Reputation

Job makes an interesting and pretty bold claim in this section: "For *when the ear heard*, it called me blessed, and *when the eye saw*, it gave witness of me." In other words, at the mention of Job's name, or at the sight of his presence, people got excited. Now what in the world would make a poor, sick widow excited to hear that Job was approaching her premises? The same thing that makes my kids excited when I walk in my front door after being gone on a trip. Not only are they excited to see me (because of course I'm awesome), but they are also excited to see what I have hidden in my suitcase. Okay, that might be a big part of it. My kids know, after many years of training, that Dad doesn't return home from a trip empty-handed.

The poor, the injured, the destitute, and the dying all know one thing about Job: they know that he never shows up empty-handed. Job had been so consistently meeting the needs of this group of people that when they saw him coming, they all got pretty excited. Job had developed a reputation for being a guy who went after needs and did what was in his power to help. This was the same kind of reputation Jesus had, and this was the same kind of reputation the early church, according to the book of Acts, had well established in short order.

I once spent a couple of years attempting to convince a friend of mine that I wanted to help her out. She was sassy, hilarious, a widow, and later in years. But even after helping her a few times, she didn't seem excited to ask. About two years after our friendship began, she called me in the middle of the night. Her furnace had exploded, and she said frantically on the phone, "I didn't know who else to call!" I was beyond flattered. With her, I had developed the right reputation.

I need to remind you again, we are talking about disciplines. We are talking about the habits of our lives that an outside observer would identify as fixtures. So here's the hard question—one that I have found difficult to even ask myself: Is there anyone in need who would be excited to see me show up *before* I ever stated the reason for my arrival? That is a tall order. It takes time and energy to develop a reputation, especially when that reputation must be developed with a group that I don't naturally spend a lot of time with. But here is the deal: a righteous man pursues mercy until his reputation for doing so precedes him. There is only one way to get there, and that is to start. Make God proud, dive in, and don't look back. Do not quit. Maybe someday you will be lucky enough to get a late-night phone call.

Making It Happen

> For when the ear heard, it called me blessed, and when the eye saw, it gave witness of me, because I delivered the poor who cried for help, and the orphan who had no helper. The blessing of the one ready to perish came upon me, and I made the widow's heart sing for joy. I was eyes to the blind and feet to the lame. I was a father to the needy. (v. 11–13, 15–16a)

(Write down your answers, and discuss them with a likeminded guy.)

What obstacles have kept me from pursuing mercy and striving to develop a reputation among people in need?

What do I need to do to overcome these obstacles?

What practical steps am I going to take to implement this discipline into my own life?

Prayer: God, give me the confidence to pursue mercy and the opportunities to meet needs. Give me the courage to overcome any obstacle that stands in my way and the determination to make it happen.

Execute Justice

The Seventh Discipline

> I put on righteousness, and it clothed me; my justice was like a robe and a turban and I investigated the case which I did not know. I broke the jaws of the wicked and snatched the prey from his teeth. (Job 29:14, 16b–17)

Yeah ... It is getting pretty serious. The metaphor Job chooses to describe his understanding of righteousness and justice is clothing. For Job, these ideas were of practical consequence. He didn't just carry righteousness and justice inwardly as ideals of the mind and heart. No. Not Job. He is essentially saying that his righteousness and justice were like his mask and cape. This is the first mention of a superhero outfit. The discipline of pursuing mercy involves, for the most part, invisible enemies—illness, poverty, loss, and death. These shadow enemies are impersonal. But the discipline of executing justice involves real people who through their actions have made themselves the enemies of righteousness and justice. Executing justice is the decision to take sides between two parties and allowing righteousness to determine which side to take. If pursuing mercy puts a person in awkward situations, executing justice only takes awkward and adds in a little crazy. When you start actively standing up for people, it can get a little intense.

It's probably important to remind you before we explore this subject that you are not law enforcement. Unless of course you actually are. But for the rest of us, we should not act like we are some undercover league of SWAT team wannabes. Doing so will get you into trouble in most places. This will require you to keep your mental fantasies in check.

As a teenager I woke one night to the sound of voices in the house. Naturally, I grabbed a baseball bat and headed down the stairs to confront these intruders. The intruders were a group of blind children connected to my parents' ministry who were sleeping the night in our living room. Crisis averted. When I told this story later, my family asked, "Did it not occur to you to wake someone else up?" Nope. It did not cross my mind. Never mind that I had a house full of family members; my mental script only called for one hero and no sidekicks. This is not being a hero. This is being an idiot. As we examine this discipline, let's be heroes, not idiots. If you are going to master the very challenging skill of executing justice, it will require three commitments.

Commitment 1
Show Up and Be Present

One of my favorite moments as a parent is to walk into a room of my house where a few of my kids are and have all motion and sound in the room cease at my arrival. I stand in the doorway while my kids stare at me, silent and motionless. This only happens for one reason: my kids are up to no good. The basic principle is this: many people will cease their bad deeds if someone who doesn't agree with their actions just shows up at the door. The reason my kids cease their behavior upon my arrival is because my kids know I stand against all plots to dismember toy dolls for no reason. They know I stand against such senseless destruction regardless of how much the doll deserved it.

The examples of this kind of ministry are a bit difficult to include in a book like this because of the sensitive nature of the stories involved. There have been times where a conversation based upon a hunch landed me in a courtroom, an attorney's office, or at police headquarters. I have been threatened and told I was meddling with something that was none of my business (weird that abusers think they are entitled to privacy), and I have even had my life threatened on a couple of occasions. But here's the deal: in many of these situations, my primary role was simply to be present and make my presence known. "Just so you know, I am here, and I know what is going on." It is amazing how cowardly evil can be when righteousness walks in the door.

The story of the woman caught in adultery is a good example of this (John 8). In this instance there was a life on the line. Amazingly, Jesus didn't really do anything. He asked a simple question that made known where He stood on the matter … and no one present was willing to continue with their plan with Him standing there. He didn't intervene, but His presence ended the matter. Those evil men proved themselves to be the cowards they really were.

Sometimes executing justice is as simple as being present where injustice is about to go down. And then other times more is required.

Commitment 2
Dare to Get Involved

Throughout my college days in Chicago, I rode the Red Line L Train to and from school each day. On numerous occasions I saw a scam unfold involving a man with a ball and caps routine. He would arrange three caps on a clipboard. Under one was a small ball. The goal was to track which cap the ball was under as he quickly and deceptively rearranged them. You know which game I am talking about. The scam, however, was that the guy always had three secret accomplices who would initially win money and then very enthusiastically convince other gullible riders to play as well. I saw one man lose $100 in under two minutes.

On one particular afternoon I was with my wife returning from church in the suburbs, and four scammers boarded our train. After the usual routine of the overly jubilant secret accomplices, I noticed two obviously naïve not-very-city girls in their teens about to jump in. One of the two girls whipped out what looked like about $500 in cash. I assumed this was probably shopping money for their trip into the city. Everyone else on the train looked the other direction. There was apparently no other justice-turbaned, evil jaw–smashing people on that train. I looked at my wife, shook my head, and said "I'm not letting this go down."

I got up from my seat, walked down to where they were, and said very simply, "This is a scam. All of these guys are working together, and you need to put your money away." I had anticipated some disappointment on the part of the scammers. I had not anticipated the rage and the ensuing litany of threats that followed. It made for an awkward train ride. These crooks didn't care that I was present at all. But once I was involved, their whole operation was exposed and temporarily brought to a halt.

No different than in the day of the traveling medicine men, today many people are being taken by sophisticated scams and often lose a lot of money. People become so emotionally invested in these scams it becomes nearly impossible for them to see reality for what it is. Queen Esther was caught up in one of the greatest scams ever recorded. A wily politician named Haman had used his manipulating skills to get irrevocable permission to wipe out the Jews. What Haman didn't realize was that the queen of the land was also a Jew. Instead of jumping to action in defense of justice, Esther hesitated out of fear for her own life.

Esther's uncle Mordecai was not impressed. "Do not think to yourself that in the king's palace you will escape any more than all the other Jews. For if you keep silent at this time, relief and deliverance will rise for the Jews from another place, but you and your father's house will perish. And who knows whether you have not come to the kingdom for such a time as this?" (Esther 4:13b–14)?.Mordecai did not mince words. "You have an opportunity to execute justice; now do it!"

Fear is always a factor when it comes to stepping into someone else's human drama. There was one opportunity I missed over a decade ago that still haunts me to this day. I knew something wasn't right; I knew I needed to intervene, and I didn't. I was too afraid. I had not turned my conviction into a habit.

Yes you might get hurt, you might get screwed, you might get killed. Jesus did. All of the badness that you are stepping in to prevent will probably be directed at you. But evil *should* be confronted. And that's exactly what Job did. He didn't bust the jaws of the wicked because they were friendly. He busted jaws that were attempting to bite someone's head off.

Sometimes showing up is enough. I prefer that. Other times, getting involved is required. But one final commitment must guide our involvement.

Commitment 3
Remember Kindness

> He has told you, O man, what is good; And what does the LORD require of you But to do justice, to love kindness, And to walk humbly with your God? (Micah 6:8)

Execute justice. And always love kindness. And always walk humbly. Getting involved in the justice business does not mean abandoning kindness. When you get involved in crazy situations, there are usually huge and sensitive egos at play, and it is all too easy to get sucked into the foolishness as your own ego comes under attack. (Think Robert Downey Jr.'s Ironman: executing justice and acting like a total jerk.) Furthermore, it becomes very easy to feel that any level of disrespect would be deserved and even encouraged by anyone in the know. Sometimes those most willing to jump into a fight are those who love fights. We are not to love fights. We are called to love justice and to wear it like a turban but always keeping in mind that the rest of our clothing is righteousness. When people, through our actions, experience the justice God desires, they should also experience the kindness that God loves.

There is an inspiring little story hidden in the book of Jeremiah that puts flesh to what I'm talking about. The story is found in Jeremiah 38. Jeremiah had the unfortunate assignment of telling the Israelites that they were fighting a losing battle against Babylon. This of course made the army generals a little peeved as they watched the morale of their troops rapidly decline in response to Jeremiah's bleak outlook. Like any good leader would, they decided the best solution would be to toss Jeremiah into a well where no one could hear him. So with King Zedekiah's permission, they did. It's important to note that Jeremiah was no spring chicken at this point. He was a man increasing in years who was already losing his strength. And as a result of his obedience, there he sat in the mud at the bottom of a well.

But serving in the house of the king there was an Ethiopian eunuch by the name of Ebed-melech. Eb was a justice-executing kind of guy. When he heard what had happened to Jeremiah, he went immediately to the king. "My lord the king, these men have done evil in all that they did to Jeremiah the prophet by casting him into the cistern, and he will die there of hunger, for there is no bread left in the city" (Jeremiah 38:9). So the king, who was apparently a flip-flopper, changed his mind and decided to authorize Jeremiah's rescue.

Anticipating the possibility of a melee, King Zeb sent Eb with a detachment of thirty soldiers to pull the prophet from his muddy grave. On his way to be the hero, Eb stopped and grabbed two items: a rope and some rags. "Then Ebed-melech the Ethiopian said to Jeremiah, 'Put the rags and clothes between your armpits and the ropes.' Jeremiah did so. Then they drew Jeremiah up with the ropes and lifted him out of the cistern" (Jeremiah 38:12–13). Amazing— heroism in the context of surprisingly sensitive kindness. Aware of the prophet's age and the difficulty of lifting him out of the mud at the bottom of a well, Eb thought to ease the difficulty by bringing comfortable padding. This is the kind of justice God desires. Eb was prepared for a potential riot, but he was also prepared to show over-the-top kindness in the middle of a tense situation.

If you are going to develop the capacity to wear justice as a turban and righteousness as a robe, it will require you to overcome your social phobias and get involved when you sense there is foul play at hand. Many times, a person in a dangerous or abusive situation will not tell anyone out of fear of how that information will be used. But as you prove yourself trustworthy and genuinely concerned, the real story comes to the surface. It is the discipline of stepping in instead of stepping away. You can decide to investigate the case you do not know. You can decide to wear your justice and righteousness as your outer garment. Don't give up. Don't quit. But be careful, and try to avoid getting yourself killed.

Making It Happen

> I put on righteousness, and it clothed me; my justice
> was like a robe and a turban and I investigated the
> case which I did not know. I broke the jaws of the
> wicked and snatched the prey from his teeth. (v.
> 14, 16b–17)

*(Write down your answers, and discuss them with a
likeminded guy.)*

What obstacles have kept me from executing justice and involving
myself in situations where injustice is at work?

What do I need to do to overcome these obstacles?

What practical steps am I going to take to implement this discipline
into my own life?

Prayer: God, give me the capacity to learn how to wear my justice
and righteousness as clothing. Give me the courage to overcome
any obstacle that stands in my way and the determination to make
it happen.

Ready for Rough Times

The Eighth Discipline

Then I thought, "I shall die in my nest, and I shall multiply my days as the sand. My root is spread out to the waters, and dew lies all night on my branches. My glory is ever new with me, and my bow is renewed in my hand." (Job 29:18–20)

This is the first time in chapter 29 that Job hints at the possibility that he may have erred in his thinking. I know; seems unlikely! And yet it's true. Job had mistakenly believed the notion that, after achieving a certain degree of security and stability, he would press repeat and live a comfortable existence for the rest his life. "I shall multiply my days." Life was good and would continue to be. We don't know what led to this belief; whether it was experientially driven or theologically developed, we only know he had bought into it. Much of the book of Job is the story of his wrestling match over this issue. Job found it difficult to undo this false belief. He was terribly confused when this belief didn't become reality.

And it is this issue that leads us to a somewhat sticky and difficult point that is illustrated in the life of Job. While Job believed his God-honoring life had qualified him for a certain level of predictable comfort, the opposite was true. Job's God-honoring life was exactly the thing that qualified him for the suffering he endured. It would be insufficient to say that his righteousness did not save him from suffering. It would be more accurate to say that his righteousness was precisely the reason he suffered.

> The LORD said to Satan, "Have you considered My servant Job? For there is no one like him on the earth, a blameless and upright man, fearing God and turning away from evil." Then Satan answered the LORD, "Does Job fear God for nothing?" (Job 1:8–9)

The only reason Job was a topic of conversation to begin with was because he was awesome. God chose Job to prove His glory because He believed Job could handle the test. But this idea shouldn't be new to us. Isn't the same true of Jesus? Was it not His perfect obedience that qualified Him for the horrible suffering of the cross? Remember for a moment my analogy of army ranger boot camp. Those guys suffer hardship in order to qualify for what? That's right—in order to qualify for an entire career of more hardship! In fact, every year, many more apply for a chance to enter boot camp than are accepted. And they do so because through that hardship there is great honor. They know their mission is a noble one.

Paul says enthusiastically to the church in Philippi, "For to you it has been granted for Christ's sake, not only to believe in Him, but also to suffer for His sake" (1:29). Guess what? You have qualified for intense hardship for the sake of joining with Christ in His mission on the earth. And through that hardship there is great honor. Christ's mission is a noble one. And with Him, the reward is incomprehensibly great. Instead of looking for a life of comfort, we should ready ourselves for when the going gets rough.

If you are going to develop the discipline of maintaining readiness for when life gets rough, there are three commitments that will help you get there.

Commitment 1
Never Stop Dying

A Good Day to Die Hard. That was the title of the 2013 Bruce Willis flick where John McClane and son travel the world sort of trying not to get killed but sort of not caring as they take on all that is evil. I do like the title. I think the apostle Paul would have liked it as well. "I affirm, brethren, by the boasting in you which I have in Christ Jesus our Lord, I die daily" (1 Corinthians 15:31). For Paul it was always a good day to die. We don't know if he died hard or died easy; we just know he did it daily.

The concept of dying daily is one I have heard confused recently. For the believer there are three different deaths that are relevant. There is the death of Christ, which I share in by faith and through which I am eternally brought to life in spirit by His Spirit. That death was once and for all (Romans 6:10). No need for Christ to go back to the cross again and again. The second death referred to in Scripture is our physical death, which also happens only once (Hebrews 9:27). The third death—the one Paul is referring to in his letter to the church in Corinth—is the death of putting aside the raging demands of the flesh. It is the death of suffering hardship for the sake of the mission of Christ on earth. Elsewhere Paul says, "Put to death the deeds of your sinful nature" (Romans 8:13). It is saying no to me and yes to Christ. This kind of death must happen every day.

Job said, "I will die in my nest." A nest is a place of comfort and security. He is referring to a future time. I will die someday, and I will die in comfort. Job is of course referring to his ultimate physical death. But I think he is also acknowledging his false belief. There was only one time in my life that I thought, *Well, I think I will be doing this same thing for the foreseeable future.* It was my first real youth ministry assignment. I loved the ministry, and it was growing. Through a series of unfortunate and painful circumstances, I left that job with no concrete plans ahead of me. I thought my nest would be predictably comfortable, and instead I had to die daily. It was pretty rough for a period of time. And yet it was great training for me. If you are going to be ready for rough times, you need to develop the habit of dying daily. You need to learn to center every day around something other than you.

Commitment 2
Never Stop Pressing

As the captain of a small commercial fishing vessel in Bristol Bay, Alaska, for several years, it was my job not only to find fish but also to keep my crew going beyond what many might consider a normal breaking point. The salmon returning to the Bristol Bay region do so in large numbers and in a short time—tens of millions of fish in just a few weeks. This meant sixteen- to twenty-hour days for days or weeks with no break.

One of my young deckhands in particular would work and work and work and then hit a wall. His productivity would visibly plummet. He was used to pushing himself to a certain point and then stopping. What he didn't know was that this limit was self-imposed. Sure, there are real limits, but I knew he hadn't hit his.

I took him aside and explained to him, "When you feel that wall, you need to have a conversation with yourself. You need to tell yourself, 'Self, I know you are tired, but you must not quit. You must keep going. The fishing season will soon be over, and then you can rest with a fat paycheck in your hand. For now, *do not quit.*'"

I assured him that he would discover a second wind if he would push through his fatigue, and sure enough he did. There are real limits. I just don't think many of us push against them very often.

Paul said to the church in Philippi, "Brethren, I do not regard myself as having laid hold of it yet; but one thing I do: forgetting what lies behind and reaching forward to what lies ahead, I press on toward the goal for the prize of the upward call of God in Christ Jesus" (Philippians 3:13–14). When it comes to pursuing the righteous life, many push themselves to become morally upright people. But few continue to push outward into a world that desperately needs righteous men to engage it. Don't settle for becoming just a good Christian. Be like Job and become an incredibly awesome one. When you start to "grow weary in doing good," take a second and have a conversation with yourself. Tell yourself, "Self, I know you are tired, but don't quit. This life is short, and the fishing season will soon be over. Then you can rest with a fat paycheck in your hand. For now, *do not quit.*"

The commitment to lay aside what is behind and never stop pressing ahead is another way I keep myself ready for when life sends rough times. I do not enter those times flabby and out of shape. I enter them conditioned by my daily habit of pressing ahead.

Commitment 3
Never Stop Passing It On

So what then is this mission of Christ that requires us to die daily and keep pressing forward? Let me tell you a story of a guy who didn't quite understand this mission. His name was Hezekiah. You may remember him. He was one of the few kings of Israel who did a lot of things right. But he didn't do everything right. In a moment of poor judgment, he decided to show off all of his riches by taking a group of Babylonians into the inner chambers of his palace. Shortly after, along came the prophet Isaiah, and he told Hezekiah that everything he had shown the Babylonians was going to be hauled off to Babylon because of the disobedience of Israel. Naturally, Hezekiah was concerned. But only for a bit. Listen to the exchange:

> Then Isaiah said to Hezekiah, "Hear the word of the LORD. 'Behold, the days are coming when all that is in your house, and all that your fathers have laid up in store to this day will be carried to Babylon; nothing shall be left,' says the LORD. 'Some of your sons who shall issue from you, whom you will beget, will be taken away; and they will become officials in the palace of the king of Babylon.'" Then Hezekiah said to Isaiah, "The word of the LORD which you have spoken is good." For he thought, "Is it not so, if there will be peace and truth in my days?" (2 Kings 20:16–19)

Wait! What? How is it that he felt this was a "good" word from the Lord? Hezekiah felt good because Hezekiah was apparently not terribly concerned about events beyond the scope of his own life. As long as these bad predictions didn't happen while he was around he was okay with it. Hezekiah was quite cozy in his nest. And apparently that was the end of the matter. But it wasn't the end. Hezekiah's son Manasseh turned out to be the most awful king in Israel's history.

Hezekiah failed to fill his later years with passing it on, and the whole of the nation Israel suffered as a result. What if Hezekiah, instead of settling down comfortably for the duration, had plunged head first into the mission of making a disciple of his own son? What if he had effectively passed it on? But of course passing it on takes a lot of work. And who needs that kind of work when there is no immediate threat? Are you catching this? Hezekiah retired. He hung up his gloves. "My glory is ever with me." He settled for comfort and security in his time. Hezekiah did not ready himself for rough times because the rough times would come after his death. He was too short-sighted.

Job was part of God's eternal work and plan on earth. His life and suffering were to be a force for good, generations after his death. You are a part of God's eternal work and plan on earth. Your life is meant to be a force for good, generations after your death. But this will require you to die daily, to press ahead, and to pass on the good news to those who will pass it on to others. This is called disciple making. It's multiplication; God's plan for mankind since the very beginning (Genesis 1:26–28). It is multiplying all of God's goodness toward me into the lives of others.

And it is hard work. If you decide right now that your life is not about you (dying), that you are not going to settle for what you have already achieved (pressing ahead), and that you are going to commit yourself to passing on your faith through word and deed to others (disciple making), I am confident you will not waver when the going gets rough. Not only will you make it through boot camp, but you will be successful in your future missions. Don't make the mistake of Job. Don't settle for comfort and security. Don't quit now. Whatever hardship you face will be worth it. The fishing season is almost over. And then you can rest with a big fat paycheck in your hand.

Making It Happen

> Then I thought, "I shall die in my nest, and I shall multiply my days as the sand. My root is spread out to the waters, and dew lies all night on my branches. My glory is ever new with me, and my bow is renewed in my hand." (v. 18–20)

(Write down your answers, and discuss them with a likeminded guy.)

What obstacles have kept me from accepting the challenge of suffering in order to join Christ in His mission?

What do I need to do to overcome these obstacles?

What practical steps am I going to take to implement this discipline into my own life?

Prayer: God, give me the foresight to ready for hardship as I commit to join You and Your mission. Give me the courage to overcome any obstacle that stands in my way and the determination to make it happen.

Speak Wisdom

The Ninth Discipline

To me they listened and waited, and kept silent for my counsel. After my words they did not speak again, and my speech dropped on them. They waited for me as for the rain, and opened their mouth as for the spring rain. I smiled on them when they did not believe, and the light of my face they did not cast down. I chose a way for them and sat as chief, and dwelt as a king among the troops, as one who comforted the mourners. (v. 21–25)

On one particular road trip during my childhood overseas, I thought it would be a humorous passing of time to try and throw items from my window and hit pedestrians along the road side. Unlike American interstates, the highways there often became very narrow as they wound through small towns, bringing my targets within easy shooting distance of my back-row seat.

Needing to up the thrill ante, I decided a cup of water would be a great next step. When the right moment presented itself, I unloaded that cup on a construction worker in a ditch right on the roadside. Perfect hit. I felt the joy of accomplishment.

But my enjoyment of the moment was quickly jarred by the sound of my brother's voice two rows ahead of me in the family van: "Ha, ha, that was funny! Aaron just threw a cup of water on that guy's head!"

This was immediately followed by the sound of the van tires screeching to a halt. I'm not sure that my dad even pulled out of his lane. "Did you dump water on someone's head?"

Suddenly it all sounded so serious and sort of evil. I was so stunned by the sudden exposure I'm not sure I answered, but surely my face told the story. "Go back right now and apologize."

So I did. It was awkward. I slinked back into my seat, and nothing was said until we arrived home. My dad asked me to wait in my room until he was ready to talk with me. So I did. And it seemed like forever. I assumed he needed additional time devising a very sophisticated and elaborate form of discipline that would probably last a lifetime. But he wasn't. He was finding the words to say. When I finally received the word that I was to meet him in his home office, I wanted to go puke instead. I sat down in a chair, and he opened his Bible to Matthew 25:44–45:

> "Then they themselves also will answer, 'Lord, when did we see You hungry, or thirsty, or a stranger, or naked, or sick, or in prison, and did not take care of You?' Then He will answer them, 'Truly I say to you, to the extent that you did not do it to one of the least of these, you did not do it to Me.'"

My dad then explained to me that because Jesus cares about every person, He takes it personally when we either help or harm others. And then he dropped the bomb: "When you threw that cup of water on that man, it's just like throwing a cup of water on Jesus." I was speechless. I didn't want to throw a cup of water on Jesus. But I knew he was right.

One of the most deeply engrained Western culture male stereotypes is that men are bad with words. Think Kronk from *The Emperor's New Groove*. But using words well is not about increasing quantity and tempo. In fact, talking a lot and talking fast are associated with using words poorly. "Do you see a man who speaks in haste? There is more hope for a fool than for him" (Proverbs 29:20). Using words well is using words for the right purpose. And it usually doesn't take a lot. If you feel verbally incompetent because the right words don't come quickly or in large quantities, you can rest at ease. You can master the art of speaking wisdom.

You have probably heard the saying, "Actions speak louder than words." And I think it is true. In fact, actions are the main point of this little devotional you have been reading. I think there is reason this part of Job's description is saved for the end. Without the detailed report of his righteous actions, this section on the weight of his words would surely seem a bit shallow. But I would like to improve that well-known saying with a better one: "Words illustrated by actions speak loudest." Words do matter, and they matter a lot. The best option is that I love my wife in word and in deed. God loves us in word and in deed. He shows us love and then tells us about His love so we can understand it.

In that one brief conversation with my dad, I grasped why he had given his life to help blind Filipinos. He did it because of His love for Jesus. His actions had been preaching, but His patiently chosen words of wisdom explained it best. The following three commitments will help focus your efforts to develop the discipline of speaking wise words.

Commitment 1
Master Words that Matter

"After my words they did not speak again." I find the modern format for cable news shows to be particularly obnoxious. I like watching the news until they say something like, "And now we have so-and-so and another so-and-so to weigh in." What they really mean is, "And now we are going to have a three-way yelling match where we ignore each other and all talk at once, making it impossible for you to decipher a word we say." It's worse than bad manners. It's words that don't matter. They are talking to be seen talking, not because they have something valuable to say.

Apparently Job had a way of speaking that ended the debate. Notice that there was silence on either end of his statements. "To me they listened and waited, and kept silent for my counsel. After my words they did not speak again." You don't get the impression that he was so desperate to be seen speaking that he would blurt out his thoughts on top of what was being said. Not Job. Because Job's words mattered so much to him, he would not spend them cheaply. Because Job's words mattered to others, they were carefully considered.

The pathway to accumulating a database of words that matter is not complicated. "Pay attention and listen to the sayings of the wise; apply your heart to what I teach, for it is pleasing when you keep them in your heart and have all of them ready on your lips" (Proverbs 22:17–18). If you want the ability to use words that matter, get in the habit of listening. You can learn a lot by listening. Get yourself around a wise person you respect and then let him or her talk. Another good way to listen is to read the Proverbs. Listen to the written words of wisdom. At the right time, they will be ready on your lips.

As you gain wisdom, become strict about when and where you share it. "A prudent man keeps his knowledge to himself, but the heart of fools blurts out folly" (Proverbs 12:23). If you want your words to matter, don't use them cheaply. I find this most difficult with my kids. I tend to blurt out my instructions while we are both still worked up. These kinds of words don't really matter. A better plan is to wait, like my father, until I have the words and I know I have a receptive audience. Because what I have to say matters, I will wait until my child is ready and willing to listen without incessant arguments.

Commitment 2
Master the Craft of Counsel

"And kept silent for my counsel." One year while out moose hunting with my older brother, we had our first encounter with a grizzly bear. (We've had more since then.) We spent over an hour hiking from our camp to a hard to reach spot and settled in to try our moose calling for the evening. After about an hour of calling, we noticed a grizzly making its way across the swamp parallel to us about seventy-five yards away. We didn't want to blow our chances with the moose by making a bunch of noise, so we stood up and made ourselves visible by waiving our hands in the air like a couple of goons.

Eventually the bear laid eyes on us. After assessing his situation for bit, he decided to skedaddle. We watched the bear run the length of the swamp away from us and then listened as he ran through the trees, trampling the underbrush beyond our ears reach. There wasn't time to relocate and so we settled back down and began our moose calling again. About two hours later, after no response from Mr. Moose, Mr. Grizzly reappeared. But this time we didn't see him coming. That bear had walked about a mile-long loop to sneak up on us from the opposite direction without being seen. When my brother Jason first saw him, he was less than twenty-five yards behind us and coming our way. This time we didn't work hard to keep quiet.

In less than a split second, we both jumped up, chambered a round in our rifles, and began shouting for the bear to leave. For those not up on their bear facts, a bear in full possession of its capacities is able to cover one hundred feet in two seconds. We were less than seventy-five feet from him. One one-thousand, two—chomp. We would have the opportunity to discharge our weapons once, maybe twice. That might be enough; it might not. Shooting too soon might only injure and incite the bear; shooting too late means lights out. So there we were, ready to shoot the bear but not wanting to have to shoot the bear and quite confident that the opportunity to shoot the bear was going to be very brief should he decide we were dinner. As I examined this bear's eye color through my crosshairs, I repeated one request to my older and more experienced brother, Jason: "Tell me when to shoot. Tell me when to shoot."

Truth be told, many men at different times, find their lives in a state of emergency. Even though the situation has been developing around them for some time, it feels to them like a sneak attack. Maybe a marriage is about to come unraveled, and the husband is pressed against a tree with no margin for error. He realizes that any decision could be a bad one, and no decision could be worse. The situation is paralyzing. If there was someone standing next to him that he trusted, he would be repeating the same question; "Tell me what to do. Tell me what to do."

"Gold there is, and rubies in abundance, but lips that speak knowledge are a rare jewel" (Proverbs 19:15). It's an unfortunate truth and yet it's true. The world lacks men who can speak knowledge to desperate people. But you can learn to. All great men do. Learn the craft of counsel by applying your heart to wisdom. "A wise man's heart guides his mouth, and his lips promote instruction" (Proverbs 16:23). My brother only gave me two words of instruction: "Not yet; not yet."

We faced off with that big man-eating brute for what seemed like about twenty-seven years, the trigger going from icy cold to warm and moist under my finger. The bear carefully weighed his options. Finally, slowly, one paw at a time, he turned away, and once he had his back to us, he charged back into the woods. We would all live to see another day. Master the craft of wise counsel and you will save many to see another day.

Commitment 3
Master the Courage of Comfort

"As one who comforted the mourners." Once you have mastered words that matter and are able to counsel others (which will require much effort over time), then you are ready for the hardest words of all—words of comfort. That's right—knowing what to say when the other person is bawling his or her eyes out. I don't know about you, but I find that kind of situation to be rather terrifying. The more tears that flow, the less competent I feel with my words.

On the one hand, "Pleasant words are a honeycomb, sweet to the soul and healing to the bones" (Proverbs 16:24). On the other hand, "Like one who takes away a garment on a cold day, or like vinegar poured on soda, is one who sings songs to a heavy heart" (Proverbs 25:20). So there is a right way and a wrong way to comfort someone in distress. Let me offer some advice.

The key to offering comfort is empathy. Empathy is the ability to enter into another man's experience and see his situation from his perspective without passing judgment. Job says, "Have I not wept for the one whose life is hard? Was not my soul grieved for the needy?"(30:25). That's empathy. Not that there is never a time to pass judgment, but it's usually not while attempting to comfort.

To communicate empathy, you need to acknowledge the other person's emotional state and the circumstances driving it. The basic formula is, "You feel _____, because of _____." Oftentimes men offer comfort by attempting to cure the other person of his or her emotions. "Don't feel bad …" Instead of attempting to rid others of their emotions, try acknowledging the reality of their emotions. "I know you must be pretty sad about losing your job. That's pretty rough." Notice in that one statement there is an acknowledgment of the guy's emotions and the circumstances driving them. You're communicating that you get what the person is going through.

As a young youth pastor about to walk away from a ministry position I loved, I stopped by to visit a couple of guys from my youth group at their home. Just before I left, their dad, whom I had known for some time, spoke to me. "I just want you to know that what is happening at our church doesn't define you. I realize it has been difficult, but you are a gifted man with a great future ahead of you." My conversation with him lasted maybe two or three minutes. And yet those words carried me for weeks. This was a man who had the courage to comfort. You can develop this courage too.

Your best bet for becoming a man who speaks words of wisdom is to read the book of Proverbs—not just because it contains a lot of wisdom but because it talks a lot about words. Read the chapter of Proverbs that corresponds to the day of the month and you'll read through it in a month. Repeat that every month for the next twenty years. Remember, the development of this discipline will not come easy. According to James 3:2, if you can control your words, you can control anything. Speaking wisdom is ultimate mastery. You can decide that you're just not good with words and quit trying. Or you can do the hard thing and buckle down until you master your own mouth. I say don't quit; keep working at it. So what if you embarrass yourself a few times? It will be worth it.

Making It Happen

> To me they listened and waited, and kept silent for my counsel. After my words they did not speak again, and my speech dropped on them. They waited for me as for the rain, and opened their mouth as for the spring rain. I smiled on them when they did not believe, and the light of my face they did not cast down. I chose a way for them and sat as chief, and dwelt as a king among the troops, as one who comforted the mourners. (v. 21–25)

(Write down your answers, and discuss them with a likeminded pal.)

What obstacles have kept me from embracing the discipline of speaking words of wisdom to others?

What do I need to do to overcome these obstacles?

What practical steps am I going to take to implement this discipline into my own life?

Prayer: God, give me the capacity to learn the ministry of speaking words of wisdom to others. Give me the courage to overcome any obstacle that stands in my way and the determination to make it happen.

Fulfill Covenant

The Tenth Discipline

> I have made a covenant with my eyes; how then could I gaze at a virgin? (Job 31:1)

So you may notice that we have left Job 29 and jumped ahead a bit. But if you honestly thought you were going to make it through this study without talking about women, you are deceived. Because talk about women we must. But not women generally. We are going to talk about just one woman—the one you are married to. If you are not married, you may enjoy this chapter anyway. If you are married, you will enjoy it even more. Unless, of course, you wish you were not married … In that case, you might not like this chapter at all. But it will help even you if you are willing to listen.

Job said in 31:1 that he had made a covenant with his eyes. He didn't tell us what the covenant was, but he did list some of the consequences of that covenant, the first of which was an unwillingness to gaze at a virgin. You probably know all about gazing. He then listed a few more consequences in 31:9–12.

> If my heart has been enticed by a woman, or I have lurked at my neighbor's doorway, may my wife grind for another, and let others kneel down over her. For that would be a lustful crime; moreover, it would be an iniquity punishable by judges. For it would be fire that consumes to Abaddon, and would uproot all my increase.

It would seem that the covenant Job made was a covenant with his wife—something like the marriage vows we make today. And it was one that he took quite seriously. *Abaddon* translated means *place of destruction.*[4] Job believed that a violation of this covenant was a crime leading eventually to his own rightful destruction. Violating this covenant was something not to do. But you are not reading a study about what not to do. This is a study of what to do. In my experience as a pastor, I have discovered that most men know what not to do. The Christian man who lurks at his neighbor's door hoping to seduce his neighbor's wife likely knows in his heart that this is something he should not do. Even the new and convenient Facebook lurking is likely to sound a mental alarm. And yet many a married man would confess "I am a little lost about what I *should* do." And if you don't know what you should do, soon you will be doing things you should not do.

It is the right set of habits that will not only diminish the likelihood that you will be the guy lurking at your neighbor's door but will also lead to the quality of marriage God intends. The marriage covenant is not about what you will not do; it is about what you will do. God doesn't want your marriage tolerable; He wants it fantastic. To get some direction in the development of the discipline

---

4   H.W.F. Gesenius, *Gesenius' Hebrew-Chaldee Lexicon to the Old Testament: 7th Edition* (Grand Rapids, MI: Baker Book House, 1997).

of loving your wife, we are going to turn to the book of Proverbs. Yes, I know, Proverbs was not written by Job. But if Job was the most righteous man on earth, it shouldn't be too much of a leap to assume he is on board with the Proverbs. Listen to the voice of wisdom:

> Drink water from your own cistern and fresh water from your own well. Should your springs be dispersed abroad, streams of water in the streets? Let them be yours alone and not for strangers with you. Let your fountain be blessed, and rejoice in the wife of your youth. As a loving hind and a graceful doe, let her breasts satisfy you at all times; be exhilarated always with her love. For why should you, my son, be exhilarated with an adulteress and embrace the bosom of a foreigner? (Proverbs 5:15–20)

The discipline of loving your wife will be developed through the following three commitments taken from three very specific instructions in this passage:

Commitment 1
Rejoice, and Again I Say Rejoice

"Rejoice in the wife of your youth." When is the last time you rejoiced in your wife? To rejoice means to express gladness or to show that you are very happy about something.[5] This is different than feeling happy about something. To rejoice is to make it known that you are happy. To rejoice in your wife is to say "I am happy, about you." And here is the best part: it is stated as an imperative!

An imperative is a command. A command is not negated by the emotional state of the subject. The Scripture says that I should not murder. If I murder someone, I should not say, "Well I didn't really

---

5   "Rejoice." *Merriam-Webster.com*. Merriam-Webster, n.d. Web. 15 Jan. 2015. <http://www.merriam-webster.com/dictionary/rejoice>.

like that person and I really felt like I wanted to murder them, so the command isn't super-relevant." It doesn't matter how I feel; the command is put there specifically so that when I feel like murdering someone, I don't murder him or her. There would be no command to rejoice in the wife of your youth if men always felt like rejoicing. The command is there because we don't rejoice. No, we gripe, we complain, we whine, and we sulk. But we are commanded to rejoice. We are commanded to broadcast gladness about our wives.

I know what some of you are thinking: *I am not glad about my wife. She is a pain in the neck. If I said I was glad, then I would be lying and that would be disobedience as well.* Let me help you out. Make a list of all of the things you don't like about the Devil. Then put a check next to the items on that list that are not true about your wife. Then rejoice in your wife because she is not as bad as the Devil.

I am being a bit facetious, but we often fixate or even obsess over the things we don't like and forget to rejoice in the things we do appreciate. This is disobedience. Your wife is not the Devil, and you have many reasons to be thankful for her. I have met men who describe their wife as the Devil when in reality she is obviously the angel of the two. In fact, no matter how great or poor you think your wife is at being your wife, she is God's primary strategy for making you into a great man. It is your response to her that is defining who you are.

Being great is about giving your life away. We covered this. Listen to the whole statement: "Let your fountain be blessed, and rejoice in the wife of your youth." In this analogy, the wife is the fountain. Rejoicing isn't really about you; it is about letting your wife be blessed. When I tell my wife, "I really appreciate that you are a generous hostess to people visiting our home," I am letting her be blessed. I am shedding light on the good she has done so that she has a tangible sense of the benefit of those good things. When I tell my friend, in the presence of my wife, "Jenny makes the best cheesecake west of the Mississippi," I am blessing my wife. Rejoicing isn't about making *me* happy; it is about making her happy. So rejoice in your wife, for her happiness. And again, I say, "*Rejoice!*"

Commitment 2
Let Her Satisfy You at All Times

"As a loving hind and a graceful doe, let her breasts satisfy you at all times." To be satisfied is to have one's fill to the full.[6] It means to satiate a need until I no longer feel that need. It is like eating until I am stuffed. And how does a man satisfy himself with his wife? By drinking "water from your own cistern and fresh water from your own well." A man satisfies himself with his wife by choosing to go to his wife for satisfaction. It's a simple concept that requires a brain adjustment for many men. If you are hungry and have grown accustomed to satisfying your hunger by eating Twinkies, then Twinkies is what you will crave. But if you have decided for a long time to satisfy your hunger with healthy meat and vegetables, then Twinkies will not satisfy you. And this gets to the heart of how your brain may need adjusting.

There is a belief that many people hold without thought or question, and that is that appetites are fixed and can only be managed. This is false. Appetites are within your power to dramatically change. And they change based upon which appetites you satisfy. The reason some men start ignoring their wives and instead watch TV is because their appetite for TV is overpowering. The appetite didn't get that way on its own; it got that way as that man began to fill that appetite to the full.

The man who is more attracted to his work than his wife will begin to more faithfully satisfy his craving for work and neglect his wife. And one day he will wake up and realize that he has no appetite for his wife. Most of the time that man will say, "I don't love my wife anymore; she no longer satisfies me." But this is a lie. The passage we

---

6   "Satisfy." *Merriam-Webster.com*. Merriam-Webster, n.d. Web. 15 Jan. 2015. <http://www.merriam-webster.com/dictionary/satisfy>

just read isn't a command to the wife to satisfy her husband; it is a command to the husband to be satisfied. A more honest assessment of the situation would be to say, "In disobedience to God's Word, I have ceased satisfying myself with my wife and am now experiencing the consequences of this neglect."

And now for the real kicker. The passage not only tells me how to satisfy myself with my wife, but it says why. "Should your springs be dispersed abroad, streams of water in the streets? Let them be yours alone and not for strangers with you." The reason you must satisfy yourself with your wife is so that your wife will never have to go find someone else who will be satisfied with her. By choosing to make your wife the object of your desire, by training your emotional, social, and sexual appetites to be satisfied in her, you are communicating to her that she is loved, she is valued, and she meets your need. And there is nothing on the planet that your wife needs more from you. Give your wife the gift of your own satisfaction by learning to find your greatest earthly satisfaction in her.

Commitment 3
Be Exhilarated

"Be exhilarated always with her love." That is an interesting command. The word *exhilarated* means "to be led astray in drunkenness, ravished."[7] We are instructed to be overcome with delight in our wives. And at a certain point in my life; this command seemed nonsensical.

About five years after my wife and I were married, we found ourselves stuck in what is probably the most common dynamic of dysfunction between husbands and their wives. Of course, at the time, it didn't seem common. It seemed very powerful, very unexpected, and very depressing. The dynamic was this: My wife would feel afraid because our relationship wasn't as close as she

---

[7]   H.W.F. Gesenius, *Gesenius' Hebrew-Chaldee Lexicon to the Old Testament: 7th Edition* (Grand Rapids, MI: Baker Book House, 1997).

wanted, and she would act on this fear by expressing anger and hurt. I would respond to this expression of anger and hurt by taking it personally and pulling away from my wife and refusing to open up to her emotionally. This would confirm her fears about our relationship, and round and round we would go. Although our relationship was very functional from most standpoints, our hope of true intimacy was slipping away.

I remember when it first struck me that I was tired of loving my wife. Because I was a young man who had worked hard to pursue a healthy relationship from the time we started dating, this was a terrifying reality. It wasn't supposed to end up this way—not for us! But I was not exhilarated. I was more like exhausted.

I have tried to imagine my response if someone had come to me and said, "Just so you know, God's Word commands you to be exhilarated with your wife." It wouldn't have mattered. I was not exhilarated. And it wouldn't have mattered because I did not realize that I had the capacity to lead my heart toward this exhilaration.

Jesus said in Matthew 6:21, "For where your treasure is, there your heart will be also." The order is important. Whatever you treasure, whatever you value, your heart will become attached to that thing. I was not exhilarated because I did not value my wife. And I did not value my wife because she was not satisfying my fleshly, ego-driven need for self-esteem as well as she once had. My exhilaration had died. Of course, I didn't realize that in the kingdom of God, death always precedes life. "Truly, truly, I say to you, unless a grain of wheat falls into the earth and dies, it remains alone; but if it dies, it bears much fruit" (John 12:24). My attraction to my wife was dying because it was rooted in her ability to make me feel good about me. And it had to die if God was ever going to resurrect our relationship in His image.

One cloudy day as I walked down the alley behind our Chicago apartment, I confessed my lack of love to God. And I heard one clear response: "So what are you planning to do about it?" And then this passage rang through my mind "For God demonstrates His love for us in that while we were yet sinners; Christ died for us" (Romans 5:8). It occurred to me in that moment that I had a choice: either accept things the way they were or choose to love my wife by serving her at all costs, even when it didn't stroke my ego to do so. That day I chose to value my wife. And every day since that day, my love for her has grown because I decided to make her my treasure. I decided, with God's help, to love like He loves and to find the exhilaration He commands.

"Rejoice." "Be satisfied." "Be exhilarated." This all flies in the face of our modern cultural mind-set. We think we would be more excited about our wives if they would try harder to be more exciting. This is a lie that becomes a crushing burden to our wives and sets us up for disappointment. Your selfish need is a bottomless pit of rotten darkness, and there is no human on the planet who can fill it.

But you can decide to fill your life with loving acts custom designed to speak your wife's unique love language. You can choose to celebrate your wife. You can choose to satisfy yourself with your wife. You can choose to be exhilarated with your wife. And it starts today when you choose, in practical ways, to value her more than you do yourself. It starts by making your wife priority number one today. If you will die to yourself, if you will humble yourself in this way, if you will treasure that woman, there will be a time in the future where you will look back and say, "I didn't know it was possible to love a woman as much as I love mine." This is the daily discipline of loving your wife.

Depending on the quality of your current relationship, this may seem like a tall order. You know what the options are. You can either give up or you can recommit yourself to fulfill your vows by arranging your life around the mission of loving your wife until death do you part. I would suggest the latter. And not because it is right—and it is—but because it is good … it is very good.

Making It Happen

> I have made a covenant with my eyes; how then
> could I gaze at a virgin? (31:1)

***(Write down your answers, and discuss them with a
likeminded guy.)***

What obstacles have kept me from developing the discipline of
faithfully and sacrificially loving my wife?

What do I need to do to overcome these obstacles?

What practical steps am I going to take to implement this discipline
into my own life?

Prayer: God, give me the grace and insight to daily love and serve
my wife. Give me the courage to overcome any obstacle that stands
in my way and the determination to make it happen.

In Conclusion

What if? How amazing would it be if as a set of recognizable habits you were led by a deep understanding of God's Word, enjoyed daily friendship with Him, purposefully gathered your family together, enjoyed God's abundance by sharing it with others, pursued honor through practical humility, pursued opportunities to show mercy to the helpless, executed justice on behalf of the oppressed, daily pressed ahead and never settled down, effectively spoke words of wisdom to others, and loved your wife in a way that reminded people of God? What would that look like? It would look like greatness. It would be awesome. You would be my hero. And God would brag about you.

You will not arrive there tomorrow. You will not develop these disciplines all at once. No one does. Now that you are done reading, the real work begins. My suggestion for you is that you pick one discipline and begin creatively implementing a plan to make it a habit. Then, once you feel like you have a handle on it, add another. You will need to revisit this devotional many times. Refuse to allow your weakness or failures to prevent you from pressing ahead. Some habits I developed and then lost and had to redevelop. So what? If I am motivated by the reward of righteousness and the example of Christ, why would I let my own humanity be a deterrent? You will fail, you will fall, but you will get back up and finish boot camp. You will it make through and become one of the elite. Narrow is the path, and few are those who find it. But you could be one of those few. To keep yourself on track, use the "Check-Up Tool" at the back of this devotional and then use it again and then again.

Before I wrap up, I want to address what I predict will be the most common complaint with what I have presented through the life of Job. Some will read this list and say, "All of this focus on doing sounds very legalistic." There are two reasons for this assessment. The first is that you struggle with legalism. Legalism is the belief that my righteousness is what gains God's approval. This isn't true. Nor will you find this message in this devotional. But if you have a tendency toward legalism, you will find yourself tempted to pursue these disciplines in order to encourage God to accept you. I assure you this takes the fun out of everything and turns it into a burden. The solution to this is to go back and study the gospel and the love of Christ—something not in the purview of this book. These disciplines are not about making God accept you; they are about enjoying God to the maximum by living an awesome, God-filled life.

The second reason you may feel this book is legalistic is because in your laziness you need some ammunition against anyone who would place any level of expectation upon you, and calling someone legalistic is basically a conversation ender. But if you are the person who doesn't want any observable, practical expectations placed on you, I have two thoughts. First, I'm surprised you are still reading! Maybe deep in your heart your realize expectations are good and healthy and you just need a push. I hope this devotional will be that push. Second, you are in good company. There will always be people who will support your lack of ambition and defend your lazy ways. God doesn't need you to live an incredible life, and neither do I. But you could. Yes, it is hard to get there. But you could.

Years ago I committed to becoming an Alaskan Job. I'm still working on it today. You can do the same. Today you can commit to becoming a great man like Job—maybe a Californian Job or Georgian Job or even a Malaysian Job. I'm sure Malaysia could use some more men like Job. Here's the deal: tomorrow you are going to wake up and your life will be over. Life is a fleeting vapor. We all arrive at the same finish line, but many will show up empty-handed (1 Corinthians 3:14–15). Decide today to live a life like Job. Decide today to live a life that matters. Decide today that with God's strength, you will be truly great. Then make that same decision every day until your last. And I'll look forward to our huge payday when we meet someday in paradise.

Study Tool

Grab your Bible, and work thoughtfully and prayerfully through the following six steps.

- ✓ *Step 1:* Pick the chapter of Proverbs that corresponds with the day of the month.
- ✓ *Step 2:* Before you read, pray in faith that God would speak to you, and let Him know you are willing to listen.
- ✓ *Step 3:* Read through the chapter and pick the one verse that stands out the most in your mind.
- ✓ *Step 4:* Write out the verse that you picked on another piece of paper.
- ✓ *Step 5:* Pray and ask God, "Why did this particular verse stand out to me?" *(There is a reason, and it has something to do with something going on in your life or heart.)* Write down your answer.
- ✓ *Step 6:* Pray and ask God, "What do You want me to do in response to the verse I read?" Write down your answer. Now go and do it.

Keep in mind, this is *one* method for reading the Bible. While this will be a good starting point for some, your Bible reading will need to include other strategies. I strongly recommend *Living by the Book* by Howard and William Hendricks for some very useful additional tools.

Dad Worksheet

Get a separate pad of paper and thoughtfully write out your answers. Take your time as you go, and be honest.

1) **How has my Dad hurt, offended, or failed me?** Psalm 26:2 says, "Examine me, O LORD, and try me; test my mind and my heart.

2) **How has this affected me?** Describe your thoughts and your feelings. Psalm 139:23 says, "Search me, O God, and know my heart; try me and know my anxious thoughts."

3) **How have I responded?** What have I said? What have I done? What have I decided? Psalm 139:24 says, "And see if there be any hurtful way in me, and lead me in the everlasting way."

4) **Confess your heart to the Lord.** Acknowledge what you are sorry for and what you hope for, and thank God for being there. Psalm 62:8 says, "Trust in Him at all times, O people; pour out your heart before Him; God is a refuge for us."

5) **Forgive as you have been forgiven.** Choose to cancel the debt. Mark 11:25 says, "Whenever you stand praying, forgive, if you have anything against anyone."

6) **Release It.** Entrust the situation and any future outcomes to the Lord. Pray for your dad.

Remember, *write* out your answers. If your relationship with your dad is particularly poor, you may need to repeat this process with several different issues or events. The goal is that you would resolve those issues for yourself so you can be free. [8]

---

[8]   Adapted from Fresh Start for all Nations. For more information visit http://www.freshstartforallnations.org

Family Time

The following is a list of very simple yet effective ideas for creative ways to engage your young kids:

1) **Coffee Shop Dates:** Kids love smoothies, and they really love hanging out with Dad.
2) **Bedtime Prayer:** Pray with your kids, and let them hear you tell God about your hopes and dreams for them.
3) **The Invention Game:** Stimulate creativity by having each of them come up with a genius invention. Change it up by picking a theme: for example flying or food inventions!
4) **The Honor Circle:** At the table, have your kids describe something amazing about the person to their left.
5) **You Won't Believe:** Take turns making up fantastic stories about what happened today (best to include dragons, bears, princesses, aliens, etc.).
6) **Fill in the Blank:** Start a story, but let the kids take turns filling in all of the information as you go. Once upon a time there was a _____ named_____ who loved to_____!
7) **Solve the Proverb:** Pick one verse from proverbs, and have your kids try to figure out what it means. What is a sluggard, and why should he go to the ant?
8) **Mom Is Amazing:** Take turns sharing the most amazing thing you appreciate about Mom. Try to make her blush.

9) **It's a Mystery:** Give each child a chance to ask one weird question that they have always wondered about. Then try not to answer too quickly.

10) **Pancake Surprise:** Pancakes are the easiest thing to make and can be made in a thousand shapes and sizes. Make snake pancakes for dinner, and you'll be a hero!

11) **Mind Reader:** Pick a category like *dessert,* and have each kid secretly pick a kind, like *mint ice cream.* If two kids both pick the same kind, they both get a point.

12) **Situational Awareness:** Have your kids close their eyes and then ask specific questions about their surroundings and see who answers correctly and with the most detail.

Money Manager

If you will follow through with the steps outlined here, you will find a measure of financial freedom and peace.[9]

1. Dream a little! Make a list of financial goals. The first thing on the list should be an emergency fund so you have something to fall back on instead of going into debt. The next things on the list could be getting out of debt, a newer vehicle, or a vacation.

2. Keep track of every dime you spend for a month! Keep a little notebook in your pocket, and log what you spend divided into the categories listed below (this includes the candy bars and coffee).

3. Now total up each category. How does that compare with your income for the month? Using one copy of this form, put your current income and expenses for the month in categories.

4. Make a debt list and an asset list. The debt list should have every business and person to whom you owe and the amount. The asset list should have everything you own of value, including things that are not paid for, like a vehicle.

---

[9]   Created by Linda Engebretsen. Used with Permission.

5. Congratulations! You are very brave because between the income/expense form and the two lists you are now staring *truth* in the face, and it's very freeing to know the *truth*.

6. Now we are going to give you some *steps* to help you become more financially stable and work on those dreams!

7. Look at your income. If it is less than your expenses then consider the following: go over your expenses and see where you can spend less; look at your asset list and consider selling something and then apply the cash to debt or sell an asset that you are carrying debt on; or look for a part-time second job after you have trimmed the expense categories.

8. Look at your debt list and look at your expenses and figure out which expense you can live without, and apply that money to the smallest debt you have and gradually pay it off. What a wonderful day that will be!

9. Now we want you to make a *new spending plan* with the second copy of the form. Remember, you can only spend what you have as income. When preparing this form, remember you probably have expenses that you don't pay for every month, so keep a list of those and then you will put that money in the savings category so you will have the money when the bill comes. Also, keep your dreams in mind and start saving. Even $10 every paycheck adds up!

Monthly Income and Expense Form

Income: (paycheck, child support, gifts, etc.)   _____

Expenses:

Housing: (rent or house payment,
    utilities, cell phone, cable)   _____

Food: (food, cleaning and laundry
    supplies, toiletries)   _____

Automobile: (payment, gas, maintenance
    and repair, insurance)   _____

Entertainment: (eating out, movie
    rental, childcare, lunches out)   _____

Clothing: _____

Medical: (medicine, doctor, dentist)   _____

Miscellaneous :(gifts, cash, magazines,
    barber, laundry, household)   _____

Debt: (credit card, student loans, etc.)   _____

Savings: (emergency fund, nonmonthly expenses)   _____

Total: _____

Difference: _____

Check-In Tool

This tool is a follow up to be filled out a couple of months after reading this study through the first time:

Walk with God's Light: *How have I implemented this discipline?*

Enjoy Friendship with God: *How have I implemented this discipline?*

Gather Family: *How have I implemented this discipline?*

Enjoy God's Abundance: *How have I implemented this discipline?*

Pursue Honor: *How have I implemented this discipline?*

Pursue Mercy: *How have I implemented this discipline?*

Execute Justice: *How have I implemented this discipline?*

Ready for Rough Times: *How have I implemented this discipline?*

Speak Wisdom: *How have I implemented this discipline?*

Fulfill Covenant: *How have I implemented this discipline?*

Reminder Card

As an extra reminder for those *really* wanting to gain headway, cut out this card, and place it in your wallet. Each time you pull it out, ask yourself the question, "Which of these am I developing today?"